BLUE LIGHTS AND BU
MARCUS AURF

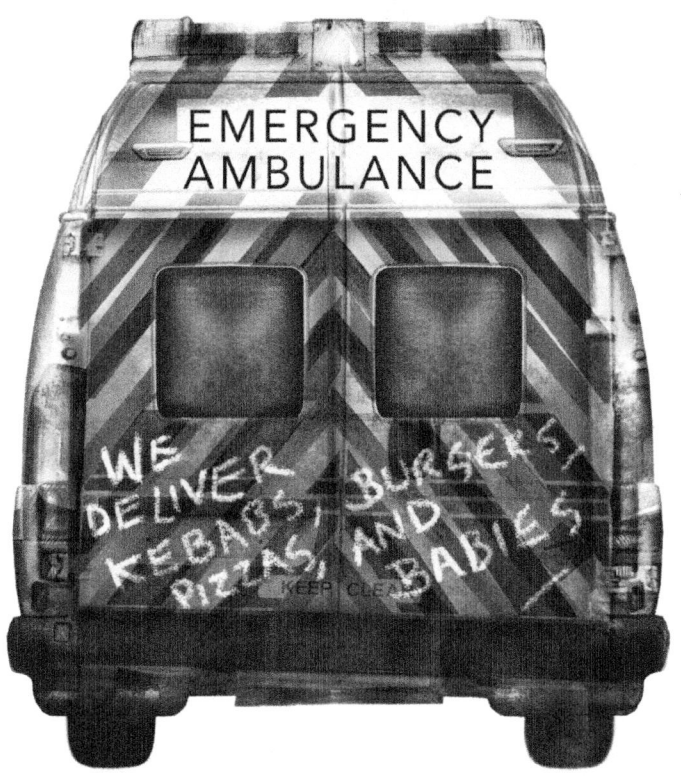

2

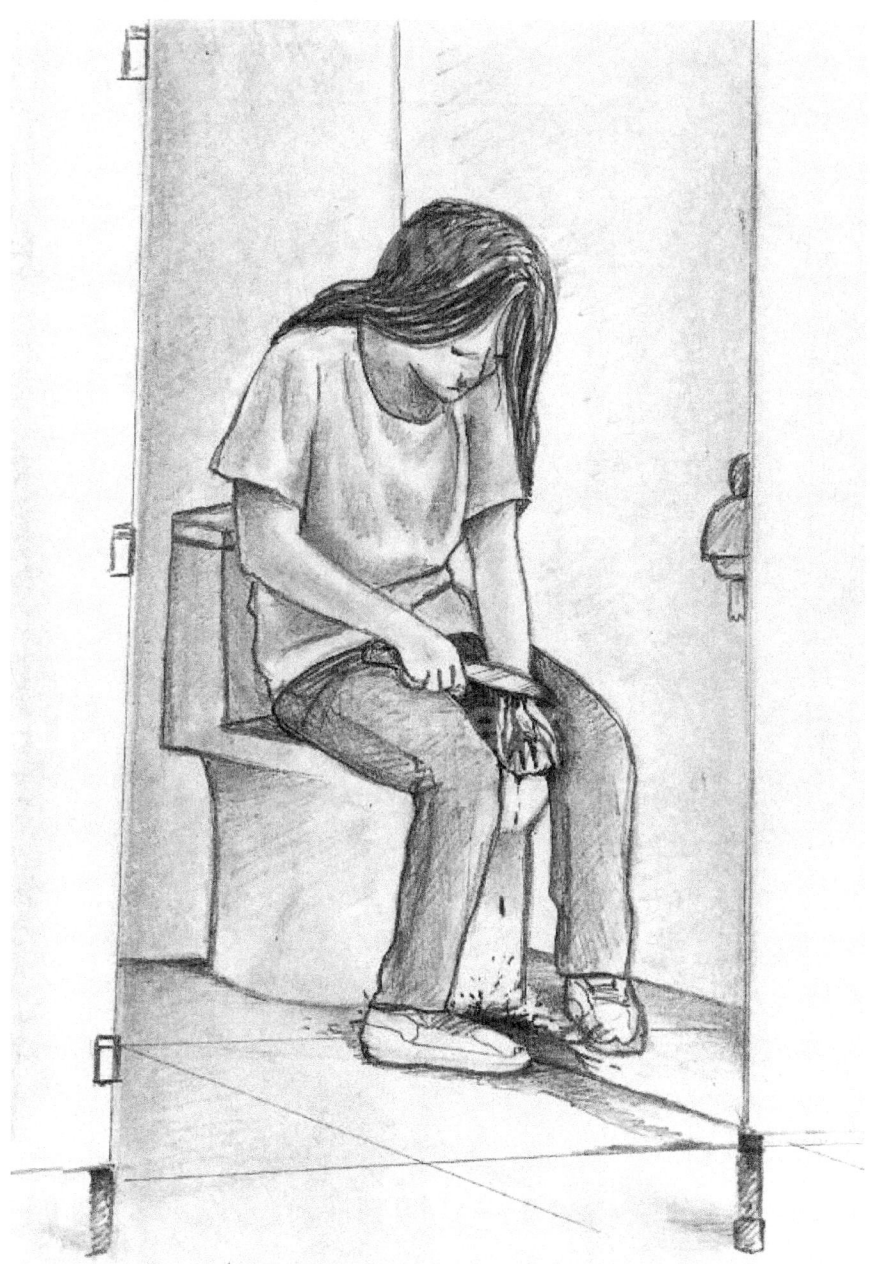

BLUE LIGHTS AND BUTTERFLIES

MARCUS AURELIUS

The sale of this book without its cover is unauthorized. If you purchased this book without a cover, you should be aware that it was reported to the publisher as "unsold and destroyed". Neither the author nor the publisher has received payment for the sale of this "stripped book."

This is a work of creative nonfiction. The events following are from the author's real- life experiences, but all names and identifying information has been altered.

Copyright © 2022 by Marcus Aurelius. All rights reserved. This book is protected under U.S. and international copyrights and intellectual property laws.

All rights reserved. Without limiting the rights under copyright, above, no part of this publication may be reproduced, stored in or reserved introduced into a retrieval system, or transmitted, in any form, or by any means (electronic, mechanical, photocopying, recording, or otherwise) without the prior written permission of both the copyright owner and the above publisher of this book.

ISBN - 9798800818833

Concept and Cover by KOOKY

Sketches by Dawn Larder

PREFACE

This book is about my experiences in the London Ambulance Service. I joined the Patient Transport Service in July 1989 and left after 20 years of service, in 2009. I then moved to Devon and worked in the South Western Ambulance Service, in their control room for three years, before retiring. This book is something I felt I had to do as it was always in the back of my mind. Not for fame or fortune, (fat chance) its just a story of my experiences that I felt had to be told.

My book is also an exposé of bad practices by some staff, more especially by some senior management.

Some senior managers were just there to do their basic job, without adding anything constructive from their previous twenty years' experience: they did their job in the same manner as they got out of bed every morning, and went to bed every evening. They never wanted their boat rocked in any way, by anything, or anyone. They wanted an easy life, and never seemed to worry about any of the consequences that might transpire from their lack of input.

I remember after I had completed ten years' service, I was asked to attend Head Office in Waterloo. I and six other colleagues were seen by a senior manager, who awarded us our ten-year service medal – he threw the boxed medals at each of us, thanked us, then asked us to leave. As you read this book you will view how senior management reacted to certain issues, and can make up your own mind about their commitment, value, and dedication to their jobs.

My book is about some of the calls that I attended, and include: the elderly, murder, hangings, mental illness, fires and other situations, as well as my time with the Patient Transport Service.

I hope you enjoy this small insight into a very satisfying and rewarding job – an immensely important job in our society as are the other emergency services.

I moved away from my busy Lavender Hill station in 2002. Therefore, all the emergency calls I attended, all take place during the period I worked there, and at my first station, and other stations where I worked overtime. All the calls take place in London and surrounding areas.

My book is not indicative of the majority of staff within this service. As with every organisation, there will always be bad apples – and those bad apples can infect the good ones. My book has, and each chapter is preceded with a Tanka and/or poem, a sketch or an illustration.

1 Tanka: Japanese poem in five lines and thirty-one syllables, giving a complete picture of an event or mood (Oxford English Dictionary).

I am very different to other people in that I am an I.N.F.J. and also have something called Synaesthesia. Some of my stories are told with the benefit of hindsight, and what was discovered, and heard at coroner's court, and my being an I.N.F.J. It stands for introverted, intuitive, feeling, and judging. I.N.F.J. make up 1% of the male population. 2% of the population are female I.N.F. J's.

They are sometimes called the mystic ones; I don't call myself anything. All I can say is that I am extremely hyper empathetic. But for me it can be far more, I feel people's auras. I cannot go anywhere where there are many people. I am hyper empathetic; I am aware of all my surroundings. I am extremely sensitive to the emotions and energies, of all life in the environment. My senses are so acute that I can absorb their energy, (good and bad) hear their thoughts, and feel their feelings, its awful most of the time, as most people are very unhappy, and have many problems. Its almost comparable to the reading of peoples minds, but not quite. Consequently, I go to quiet places to shop, and at the quietest times. I also tend to be alone most of the time, sit in a park, or a beach, so that I can recharge myself.

I also have synaesthesia, which has several forms. Its basic definition is the production of a sense impression, relating to one sense or part of the body by stimulation of another sense, or part of the body.

1. Lexical Synaesthesia, is when people have associations between words and taste. A person can hear the word cheese and he/she will taste cheese in his/her mouth. In fact, any and every word has an association with taste, some as I have read are not at all nice, even if the word is.

2. Mirror touch synaesthesia, is what I have. I feel what I see other people feel. If I see someone fall over and hurt themselves, then I will feel their pain, in the tops of my thighs and lower back. You can imagine

working on the emergency ambulance service, how I felt most of the time, dealing with some people with all types of pain. This form of synaesthesia also encompasses feelings, if I saw something sad, I would cry, if I saw something funny I could laugh uncontrollably, almost hysterically. I contacted the UK Synaesthesia association who arranged for me to be tested. I was confirmed with the use of a CT scanner, in which they show you film of accidents, people having injection, falls, etc. and they look at you brain reactions on the scanner.

3. Misophonia, comes from the Greek words hatred of sound, this creates adverse strong feelings in response to sounds, some everyday sounds can

produce negative emotions like anger and disgust.

4. Personification is where ordered sequences, like numbers, days of the week, letters, even the train time tables at main train stations, all have their own personalities, and/or appearances. Wednesday may be happy, with a woman wearing a pink dress. Friday could be someone young who is talking too much. Its also been reported that some people with this form see the letters, and numbers on a train timetable, as they change they see the letters and numbers cascade down like a waterfall.

5. Number form. This is where numbers automatically appear in the mind as mental maps.

Chromesthesia, is another form I have. I like this one. When you hear sounds, they can trigger colours, either in front of you, or in your minds eye. For me, this happens when I listen to music, I see wild colours, its like your very own personal light show. other people get it listening to certain accents and from the spoken word.

The artist Kandinsky had this form of synaesthesia, one of his paintings is called "yellow, red and blue, which is very interesting to look at, once you know this fact about him. I wasn't diagnosed with synaesthesia, until 1998, and an INFJ until 2002.

I will add a snippet of a poem, that can best describe what I have always been like. Its called;

Life changes.

I have always been susceptible to odd things,

 Strange phenomena,

Since I was little

I knew what was to be said,

look at someone and know them,

know their life,

I remember, I predicted over 12 plane crashes.

Between the ages of 23 – 40 "it" disappeared,

At some point in the ambulance service "it" reappeared,

I knew things I shouldn't know,

I could "feel" peoples pain,

Their grief, their sorrow,

I knew when they hurt,

and gave them comfort,

and they knew, I knew.

Contents.

1. GET ON SIT DOWN.
2. L.O.B.
3. THE ALIEN.
4. LORD
5. NAOMI.
6. TRACKS OF MY TEARS.
7. KRAZY KILLER
8. DEAD BEFORE ONE.
9. PATIENTS, STAFF, DOCTORS, AND NURSES.
10. FIRE.
11. LAST BIKE RIDE.
12. HANGINGS, SUICIDES, SELF HARM.
13. GOD IN THE AMBULANCE SERVICE.
14. PRANKS, DRINK, DRUGS, SEX.
15. SURFIN IN MORDEN.
16. BOY WITH THE MOON AND STARS.
17. THE FORGOTTEN.
18. ROAD TRAFFIC COLLISION.
19. WORST DAY SHIFT.
20. WORST NIGHT SHIFT.

EPILOGUE.

LIST OF DRAWINGS AND ILLUSTRATIONS.

1.	MY AMBULANCE
2.	L.O.B. JOINT
3.	L.O.B. TONGUE
4.	PAEDO
5.	LORD
6.	BABY IN VAC
7.	NAOMI
8.	NAOMI'S MUM HANGING
9.	WOMAN JUMPING IN FRONT OF TRAIN
10.	YOUNG MAN ON TRACK
11.	KILLER
12.	BABY CLOCK
13.	DEAD BABY ILLUSTRATION
14.	MAN WITH BAYNOT
15.	LOST PATIENT
16.	E.C.G.
17.	OLD MAN IN CHAIR
18.	BURNT BABY
19.	BURNT MOTHER
20.	BOY ON BIKE
21.	BOY UNDER LORRY
22.	C.C.J.
23.	SELF HARM ILLUSTRATION
24.	BODY CUTS
25.	MURDERING A PATIENT
26.	SEX IN AMBULANCE
27.	AMBULANCE TURNING WRONG WAY
28.	DAMAGE BY SPINAL BOARD
29.	BOY WITH MOON AND STARS
30.	BOOK CLUTTER
31.	OLD MAN DREAMING OF RELEASE

32. CAR V LORRY
33. GLORIA
34. LITTLE AND LARGE
35. STABBED IN CAR
36. WOMAN PULLING HAIR
37. CAR ON FIRE

LIST OF TANKAS AND POEMS.

1. GET ON SIT DOWN
2. WEIRDO PAEDO
3. LORD
4. VACUUM
5. NAOMI
6. THE WITNESS
7. KRAZY KILLER
8. DEAD BEFORE ONE
9. PATIENTS, STAFF, DOCTORS, AND NURSES
10. FIRE
11. LAST BIKE RIDE
12. ONE K
13. SOMETIME SOON
14. HELP ME PLEASE
15. BOY WITH THE MOON AND STARS
16. THE FORGOTTEN
17. LOOK CLOSER NURSE
18. SHAKE, RATTLE, AND ROLL.

Acknowledgements

Little did I know that a book was being constructed in my head on a daily basis. I'm sure some of my memories were due to PTSD (Post-Traumatic Stress Disorder). The information remained in my head, stored and shelved in sections, waiting for the moment to be collated and possibly released in the form of a book.

I went through a long period of illness when I was very ill, and because of my illness I sought refuge in college, attending as many courses as I possibly could. It was a way of passing time, in a more positive setting; a form of therapy. I took this advice from a previous work colleague, Felicity Leicester, and enrolled on a twelve- week writing course, as well as courses in film-making, photography, Photoshop, InDesign and several art courses.

My writing tutor was Sarah O'Hanlon. She was pure inspiration, never pushing, only probing and praising. Sarah would give up her own time to read what I had written, and this she did for all her students. Other students in her class charged and encouraged me to complete my project, as I did them. The course took many turns, and I thank Sarah for introducing me to Japanese poetry, as well as other forms of verse.

I would also like to thank Dawn Marie Larder for her sketches. These were born and created in my head and brought perfectly to life by her. She is from the Glimmertwin Art House, and I would gladly recommend her.

Lastly I want to thank my Missy and my Dotty. They, above all others, will never know how much they have helped me

and saved me from myself.

A special thank you to Sonia Mitchell for assisting me in formatting the book ready for printing.

Introduction

I began to write the book in 2009. I wrote one chapter and could do no more, despite being able to recount 99 per cent of the jobs I had attended. In my mind's eye I could see every serious job, as well as all the wasteful jobs, we had to attend. I could recount the date, time of day and all the people involved ... as well as the outcome. Maybe it's the same for all emergency staff, or was this the effect of PTSD? Was I different from other staff in this respect? Maybe I found it cathartic; it was something I needed to do, to free myself of some of the feelings and thoughts that I still held, although I now believe they will remain with me forever, as I can still see some of the people in my minds eye.

Everything in this book is true, although there may be some embellishment to some of the stories for the benefit of the reader. I have changed names, descriptions, places and dates to ensure anonymity. The M.P. that I wrote about in one of the stories is long dead, although I still do not recount the name. This book is not an in depth look at the ambulance service, its staff, or its procedures. It is a book that in my view covered jobs that I found sad, heart wrenching, or any number of other reasons. The jobs do not reflect a typical day's work, it is rare to be given more than 2 serious jobs in one shift, although it can happen.

This covers stories of murder, sexual assault, the

mentally ill, maternity, and of course some stories of hospital staff, and ambulance crews. Some of which I hope you find amusing, and some you will find are horrific. This is a book that I believe should be read by all, but not because I wrote it, more because it is truthful.

Get on, sit down, shut up

Get on,

sit down,

 and shut up,

Get on sit down, Shut up,

Get on, Sit down, And Shut up.

1. Get on, sit down, shut up

I started on Patient Transport Service (PTS) July 1989, and I loved it. We had three categories of patient: walkers, chairs and stretchers. We attended to the elderly and infirm, and those that needed an ambulance to get to their hospital appointments. I met lots of interesting people. Some had great stories to tell; all of them, without exception, were very nice people. Some had experienced the World Wars – some were women, who'd worked in the munitions factories.

All had something to say ... and I listened to them intently. I never got bored of their life stories and so my work was made easier and more interesting.

If my patients weren't ready when I called, I would make them a hot drink and have a chat. I would wait for them, unlike other transport staff, who hassled them. Some crews would even leave them and mark it down as a lost journey. As a result, the patients might miss their routine appointment, even though it may well have been important for them to see the doctor, or attend a clinic.

These members of staff did not comprehend the consequences for everyone. Even for ourselves. The more lost journeys we had, the more it could jeopardise our jobs in the future

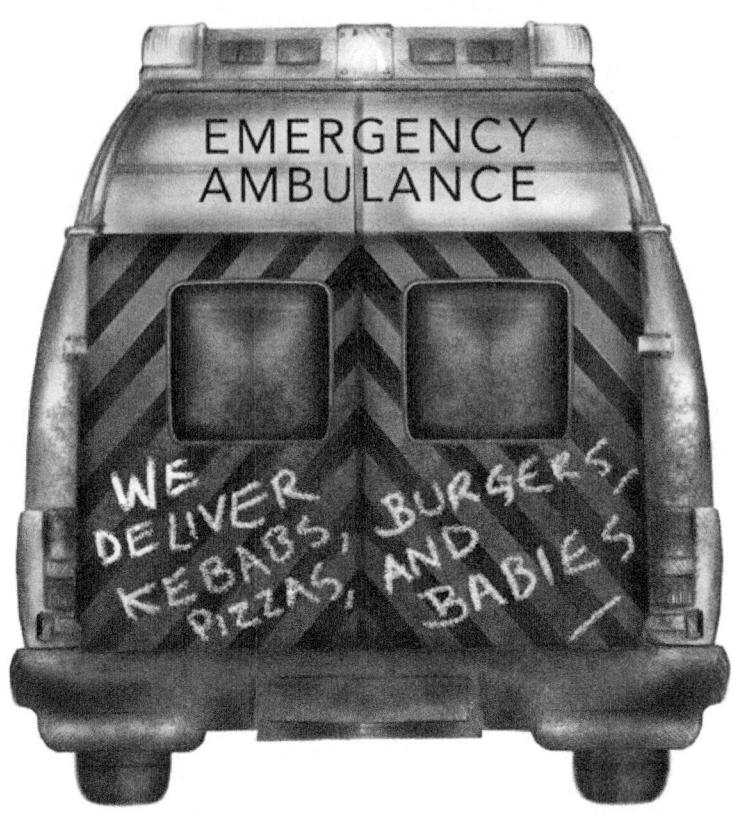

I would behave in exactly the same way on the return journey. I would give them time, put the kettle on for them and turn the heating on. Then I would leave.

My partner and I would often work fourteen-hour shifts, in order to make sure everyone got home from the hospital. If there wasn't anyone working, then the patient transport manager would have to arrange cab journeys for them, or arrange for A&E staff to take them home.

It really was a great and rewarding job, but not financially.

We would get the long journeys from various hospitals around London:

from Great Ormond Street, to take a child home for their last Christmas; or an aunt, who didn't have long to live, and wanted to spend the rest of her life with their relatives.

We made a difference. Sally and I worked all sorts of hours, which impacted on our family lives.

One lady that Sally and I would collect had just been diagnosed with cancer.

We got to know Iris really well. She would often bring us cakes that she made. During the Second World War she had held a high position in one of the war buildings. She used to tell us interesting stories and became a friend, like an aunt. We were both very fond of her.

We saw her travel as a 'walker', then within 3 months she became a 'chair' patient – cancer saw to that. After nine months she became a 'stretcher' case. It was heart- breaking to see.

In the end we took her to Trinity Hospice, a beautiful place; a place to go to die. It had beautiful gardens and was staffed by brilliant, beautiful, caring people.

We took Iris there one Monday afternoon in December, near Christmas. I can't remember the year.

It was odd to have a warm day in December. I remember I wore a short-sleeved shirt, to go to my brother-in-law's on Christmas Day, in 2001.

Iris had requested us by name, to take her from St Thomas's hospital to Trinity Hospice. We drove her and said that we would pop in before Christmas to see her.

We had flowers and chocolates for her. We knew our way to her room, and rushed up to see her.

But her bed was unmade and empty. We asked the sister where Iris was, and was told she had died early that morning.

I couldn't believe how we both cried. It felt like losing a close relative, a very good

friend.

That was the day we both decided to leave the Patient Transport Service. The thought

of watching our lovely, regular patients dying was too much to think about.

So, Sally and I decided to move on to the Emergency Service, where we would not get the chance to become too close to our patients. Maybe it was selfish, but it felt right at the time. We both left the patient transport service, and were both placed on different courses in order to be trained in emergency care. Sally did her course in London, I attended the course in Surrey. We both became emergency trainee technicians. All newly qualified staff were on probation for a year, and everyone had continuous training. After one year you had a final exam, and driving test. You then became a qualified E.M.T. (emergency medical technician). The training was ongoing throughout your career as new equipment and procedures were brought in all the time. I never worked with Sally again, she worked in South East London, I worked in South West London.

Get on. Sit down. And shut up.

That's how the job got you after five years on A&E. It took that long for the novelty to wear off.

One bloke on our station, a real 'prat the lad', actually made a sign, in cardboard with those words on it. He really was an idiot, and a member of the Territorial Army. He acted as if he had been to war, he thought he was a real tough guy, he should have joined the regular army, and not the caring profession. He was the one who later took an ambulance when drunk, just to pick up his girlfriend.

We had some blokes on station who had seen action in the Army, but they were a nicer bunch and quieter. I worked for a couple of years with one ex-soldier, who just liked to do his job. He didn't like sitting around. He never said much. One day, after about eighteen months, he opened up and started talking about his stint in Ireland. He spoke quite matter of factly. One time I asked him what he missed most about being in the Army. What he told me must have registered shock on my face, because he clammed up after that and never spoke about the Army again. He never said the usual stuff I you would hear from people who'd worked for organisations like that, like the camaraderie, the drinking and womanising, even the travelling.

When I asked him what he missed most, he actually said he missed hanging out of a helicopter with his machine gun, firing on suspected IRA terror suspects. I don't think I responded to that statement.

But back to the pretend soldier and his cardboard cut-out words. He would show his sign to patients when he was sent to an emergency call, that he deemed unworthy of getting an ambulance.

He just showed them the sign and didn't say anything. However, he was very careful who he showed it to.

We all felt like that sometimes: rushing to a worthless call, sent by our Control. You will gather in a later chapter that not all our jobs were emergencies of any type. Of course, it was still fun, driving fast, racing the idiots, who tried to beat the traffic and who impeded our progress to get to an emergency.

One day my crew-mate was driving on the wrong side of the road. We had no idea that a car had started to follow us on the wrong side of the road, right behind us. We had to stop suddenly, as a car pulled out from our right. My mate hit the brakes and suddenly we were hit from behind. The police came and the bloke had to admit what he'd done.

We weaved in and out of traffic, trying to get to the call in eight minutes, as demanded by our employer and the Government. Sometimes we drove straight at other cars, on the wrong side of the road, lights blinding them, daring them to continue on their path, and not pull over for us. We were a bit foolhardy, but it's what the job called for.

If it was a life-or-death situation you had to put yourself out, otherwise why do the job? If we got into a scrape, a minor accident, it meant we could get a bit of time off, and maybe a decent night's sleep.

God was I tired. We were all tired unlike those at Richmond Hill. Which was a quiet station. There wasn't one of us who looked well, or even healthy, especially those that had to do overtime. None of us ever slept well. When we started our shifts, we would check the vehicles, quickly have a hot drink, then close the shutters to our eyes, and try to sleep, while we could.

There was one officer who would come in at about 7 a.m. and demand that we all start doing chores: vacuuming, polishing, housework chores. I once told him I wasn't being paid as a cleaner. He still demanded we do housework. He even switched off the TV, not that any of us cared – we weren't watching the rubbish on there. We just continued our shut-eye, ignoring the little prick.

They used to run the Ambulance Service like the Army. He was from those, older times, but it wasn't like that anymore, even though some of them preferred the old ways. It's funny but the ones who had been in the Army were never like this; they were quite chilled. But others enjoyed the power they'd once had and tried to impose their authority, especially on the newbies.

Years ago, if you were new, you had to clean everyone's boots and make tea and toast and so on. That would have been enough to put lots of people off from joining any of the Emergency Services.

Those who had been in the job as long as the officer had would just tell him to shut the fuck up.

Even the amount of coffee we drank could not diminish our need for sleep. However, there was something that would – Control. We felt like they had CCTV in the mess room or they that they timed our activities: 10 minutes to do a VDI, (vehicle daily

inspection) 5 minutes to make a drink; 5 minutes to have your drink; and 2 minutes with your eyes closed.

On the twenty-third minute they would ring, and disturb our peace and tranquillity.

What made it worse was that they then put us standby. They didn't even send us to a job. We just had to sit and wait for a job,

So we went off near a major junction, or a hospital, as if Control knew where the next job would come from. Just in case we were needed. They got it wrong most of the time. They would send us in one direction and a job would come in from the opposite direction. They could not control their own bladders, let alone 350 ambulances.

I think the Service was only able to function because of our commitment, and our never-ending dedication to patients ... although that was stretched sometimes. There were weekends that were dangerous for patients, for the public and for us, through overwork.

As I've said before the Service was run on our goodwill and commitment. Everyone was entitled to annual leave, and there was always sickness and injury to consider. Crews had to cover their shifts. I remember on many occasions that Merton, Sutton and Wandsworth had a total of five ambulances to cover those areas over a weekend – Friday, Saturday and Sunday nights. The days were usually pretty well covered.

This also happened in the police force, I remember Sutton Police Station on a Saturday night having one police car, and one Special manning the station, who was a personal friend of mine.

The staff that manned our Control were okay. They weren't all bad. But some of them had no common sense. On one shift they gave us a job without any thought for the crew. We were given an urgent call to pick up a patient and take him to Tommy's (St Thomas's).

What they failed to tell us was that, on a previous occasion, he had been run over and seriously injured by one of our fast response vehicles ... on a zebra crossing. He had multiple injuries and lay in a coma for weeks. He should have died, but he lived, and he hated everything to do with the Ambulance Service, whom he had sued.

We never knew all this until we rang his doorbell, to find ourselves confronted by a mad man shouting at us and abusing us. I had never heard so much swearing from anyone in the space of two minutes. Luckily, I am calm, diplomatic and tactful, and managed to calm him down.

We sat with him in his living room, listened to his complaints, which were all valid and with which, I agreed. He and his family had been treated abominably by the Ambulance Service and its legal representatives. They had no argument: we, the Ambulance Service were to blame for his life-changing injuries.

Someone in Control should have said, 'We had better warn the crew who he is, and that he may be a problem for them.'

How stupid could they be? Why did they just not pay for a taxi to take him to hospital, and then home. The ambulance service was run on a similar system as the police, they would have addresses that were flagged up for one reason or another, and his would have been on it.

This would have saved him the anguish and anger he felt toward the ambulance service ... as well as saving us from being placed in that predicament.

The controllers also liked to play games with crews. Each sector would place bets on who could get an ambulance the furthest away from their own area by the end of shift. The sector that had a vehicle the furthest away would win the bet. It was easy for them: if one of us got to Tommy's, King's College or even Hammersmith hospitals, we would find ourselves in North London, deepest West London, (I ended up in Ealing once) or past Purley, in South London. I never found out if they played for money or just cakes, but it was a dangerous game if there was a life-or-death emergency in our own area and no available ambulance. If we were 10 miles away, the consequence could be death for someone who might otherwise have lived.

I started working in A&E at Richmond Hill Ambulance Station. It was a nice little station.

I was a 'relief', and as a relief I ended up working all the crap shifts. It was a quiet station, so time dragged, especially as I was new. All newbies were in a rush for excitement, especially if they'd watched Casualty. At Richmond Hill, I could do three or four jobs in an eight-hour shift, which the regulars there classed as 'busy'.

I could tend the garden, even watch the grass grow, cook a meal, and actually eat it without getting a call, watch TV and sleep if I wanted to – not that I needed to at such a quiet station. I was broken in gently, very gently, in this sleepy little hollow.

One night I went out with Joe. He had 12 years under his belt, was experienced and he was also an addict, addicted to Entonox, a pain-relief gas, which we gave to patients. It wouldn't kill you, but abusing it could give you brittle bones. That was a bad idea, especially in our job. It never impacted on his ability to do the job. He was still good at his job, and I felt comfortable with him. You will see later on in my book that we had staff that had addictions of all kinds, drugs and alcohol included, so his personal addiction never caused anyone any harm. He may also have been in pain, and used this as pain relief.

Our first call was to a cardiac arrest at an exclusive sports club off Roehampton Lane.

I drove. When you're new, you don't have a choice about this, especially as a relief. Also, I knew where the club was.

Control sent two ambulances, as it made sense and was easier for all of us. The place was packed, as there was a private function. All eyes were on us. The music had been turned off. There was silence in the hall, I could feel people's eyes on my back, almost piercing my skin. I heard muffled voices and women crying.

We started CPR: I did chest compressions, someone else bagged (forced air into his lungs) the patient, while another connected him to the defibrillator. The paramedic intubated our patient, so we could get a good amount of oxygen into his airway. (its only paramedics that could intubate and give cardiac drugs, at the time I

was employed. Otherwise our jobs were similar) We immediately got a shockable rhythm. He was in VF (ventricular fibrillation) when the heart stutters, shakes and doesn't do what it should do. We zapped him. And zapped him again.

Nothing.

We decided to move and loaded the patient into the other vehicle. Joe would go with them and I would convey any family or friends who wanted to accompany the patient to the hospital. A call was put in to Queen Mary's, Roehampton. We all arrived in roughly three minutes and Joe and the paramedic wheeled the patient into Resus, while I took the family into the family room.

The driver of the other ambulance – a man in his fifties who was slightly overweight – went to book the patient in. I joined him in reception. He turned and looked at me, with a quizzical look on his face, eyes glazed, sweat on his brow. He was out of breath, when there was no reason for him to be.

He collapsed, right in front of me with a cardiac arrest. I told the receptionist to get me some help and a trolley as I gave him a precordial thump (a pre cordial thump, is what you can do to a patient, if you don't have a defibrillator, you thump their chest to try and get their heart back into the right rhythm) and checked for a pulse. There was nothing. Within seconds he had joined the patient we had brought into resus. One zap with the defibrillator and he was back with the living. The patient we had brought in, unfortunately died, despite the drugs the hospital gave him.

Joe and I returned to Richmond Hill for a quick drink and sit down at the station, and watched some crap TV.
A call came in at 2200: woman screaming, baby screaming, man shouting. NFD (No Further Details). Police would be sent.

Off we went, somewhere in Richmond, and arrived in five minutes. I drove, as Joe wasn't in the mood, and I parked right outside the flat, which was above a shop. The door was wide open.

When we arrived we could hear screaming. We ventured through the door and walked upstairs.

The woman was screaming: 'He kicked my baby!' A huge man was standing over the baby like a giant.

I removed the baby gently from under this towering figure, with Joe looking on. There were needles all over the floor, everywhere. They were users, drug users. Perhaps the shouting was because they needed a fix. Maybe he wanted her to turn tricks, so that they could get their next fix.

I stopped thinking and looked at the baby.

She was becoming quieter, no longer screaming. Not a good sign.

I started to make my way downstairs. The bloke started swearing at us, not wanting us to take the baby. Joe was quite big, but the man made a move to punch my mate. Joe side- stepped him, and brought a crashing blow onto the man's exposed face, and continued to beat him, shouting, 'How do you like it, bastard!'

As I went to the ambulance. Joe left the bloke on the carpet floor, and followed me down, just as the police arrived.

They shouted to Joe to look out. The man was

coming up behind Joe with a hammer. Joe swung a punch and caught him with a nice uppercut, to the jaw, and Joe knocked him out, cold.

The police said they would put that down as 'resisting arrest'.

I put in a Blue Call (a priority call to the hospital, for a serious case.) to Queen Mary's hospital and drove like the devil. I knew the baby was in a bad way.

Tears began to well up in my eyes. I tried to turn the tap off and drove. Joe was looking after the baby. The mother hadn't come with us.

Baby was no longer crying. She was silent; a bad sign.

The druggy girlfriend had told us that he had kicked the baby like a football, then shaken her and thrown her on the floor. It made me sick just thinking about it.

We stayed at the hospital as it was nearly 'off-time' and remained there until we were informed that the baby had died. As a newbie, I was not prepared for this. This was something people read in the Sunday papers.

Joe was a nice bloke. I liked him. I heard he had disappeared from his job and his home. I think he was affected by our job, and probably the calls he had attended in the past. He probably suffered with PTSD, as I would in the near future. I remember a colleague telling me that Joe had attended a serious RTC (road traffic collision) in which a woman had been decapitated. The body was still in the car, but the head disappeared. Joe went looking for it, and 30 minutes later returned with her head in his hands, just looking at it, crying.

I worked at Richmond Hill for a year, and worked with Joe a couple more times before he disappeared. A position came up at Lavender Hill and I transferred. They did twelve-hour shifts there, with three days on and four off, then four on and three off. This suited me much better.

Richmond Hill has been quiet, but Lavender Hill was like Piccadilly Circus, with up to fifteen or sixteen jobs per shift. It was the busiest station in London, if not the country, even on Christmas Day, we were busy.

JC was my first partner at Lavender Hill. He was about 6 feet 6 inches tall and large around the middle. He didn't have long legs or arms so he looked like the Michelin Man.

Some blokes on Station compared him to a Telly Tubby. He had mid-brown hair that was never brushed or combed, deep blue eyes and was always unshaven. He looked quite scruffy: his shirts and trousers were never ironed; he rarely polished his boots. He was never loud but was a bit cocky ... and very cool. He was also very, very good at his job. If I'd had an accident, I would have wanted him to look after me, he was so good.

He was a smoker: you could always smell cigarettes on him, no matter how hard he tried to disguise it with cheap cologne. He was always in debt and had separated from his wife. This probably accounts for his appearance and his money problems.

He was always doing overtime. He worked every day off he had. On station he would always try to get some sleep and was heading for a burnout very soon.

He loved the adrenaline rush from the job; could never get enough of it. He always chased the most gruesome jobs, just for the rush.

I remember the first of many cardiac arrests with JC. It was near an industrial estate, on the other side of Wandsworth Roundabout. It was December and we were on nights. It was snowing and the roads were full of black ice. I drove and he directed me.

As soon as we hit the Wandsworth Roundabout, we hit black ice. I lost control and became a viewer, as if I was watching a film on TV. The ambulance skidded sideways at speed, towards a small wall and the River Thames. The nearer we got to the wall the smaller it looked.

I pictured the ambulance floating down the river, blue lights still on and the siren beginning to make an odd sound.

JC just sat there looking out of the window, totally unconcerned, I managed to control the ambulance the way I had been taught, but I think there was some luck in my actions. JC wasn't even looking at me; he was compelled by the excitement of my driving.

We got to the call and JC said, 'Fucking great driving.'

I smiled, little did he know what had been going through my mind.

We did what we needed to do. The patient was really big, so we seconded his co-workers to assist us. He was on the top floor and placed on our board. I started resus, while JC intubated our patient. I got him connected to the defibrillator and continued with resus. Then we lifted

him up, walked down a flight of stairs, before JC told us to stop, checked for pulse and continued resus. We did this for five flights of stairs.

Once in the ambulance JC administered drugs and we managed to shock the patient back to life. We blue-lighted him to Chelsea and West (Chelsea and Westminster Hospital), and sat there to have a coffee, while JC filled in the paperwork.

I had a lot of respect for JC, and he was very highly regarded by his colleagues. There were many like JC who craved the adrenaline rush. They would all pipe up on the radio when they heard about a 'juicy job'. But a juicy job for us meant heartache and tears for someone else. I never regarded serious jobs as 'juicy; the word was just wrong, even inappropriate.

It was just sad, and more importantly, awful for the person's family.

Crews would drive to the job from various directions, saying that they were nearer, desperate for Control to give them the job officially. They drove at full speed to an incident, racing each other, like a charging army on horseback or in chariots, screaming and shouting, music blaring, as if about to do battle – only we were going to save a life, not fight.

That was a rush in itself, madness really. We could have killed someone, or seriously hurt them, and sometimes, some of us did.

It was the nature of the job; no different from the police or the brickheads, who have injured members of the public at some time.

But we were good at our jobs, and we really did care

about our patients ... at least most of us at Lavender Hill did.

L.O.B.

Stubbed toe, cut finger

Headache, high on weed,

Make tea,

A phone call made sense

They know their rights of passage

To waste our, doctor time.

2. L.O.B (Load of Bollocks)

This chapter concerns a few of the so-called 'emergency' jobs that I have attended, which were anything but. All were jobs issued as emergencies, which had to be attended within eight minutes.

The Ambulance Service – Control, Ambulance crews, even the non-emergency '111' medical helpline – are worried about making a mistake, refusing an ambulance and consequently making more mistakes, which might leave them open to possibly being sued, because they didn't send an ambulance to a real emergency.

Or the ambulance crew that was sent never took the patient to hospital,

Or the 111 services told a patient to wait until tomorrow to see their own GP.

Everyone is afraid of making a mistake. Everyone is afraid of making a positive decision. No one said it's easy, but if you make a mistake, you have to learn from it and change, to rectify the system.

In parts of Europe, they do not hesitate to tell a patient that their illness does not require an ambulance, or that if they think they need hospital treatment, they

I Don't Care

These are some of the jobs I have attended, which had been claimed as 'emergencies':

1. Munchausen. Although this is a real mental illness, there is nothing wrong with the patient, other than the Munchausen Syndrome, which they will not die from. Some sufferers can inflict an injury on themselves, but as far as I've known its never serious. -

2. This illness is when a person pretends to be ill and fakes symptoms. Some sufferers travel to different hospitals in order to be seen, so they're not recognised. When they exhaust that

ploy, they give different names in order to get their 'fix'. I have taken a few to hospital and it's really difficult to spot a faker. I remember taking one lady to St George's, who pretended to have a grand mal seizure. She was examined, cannulated (had a needle inserted in her arm) and given drugs. It was only when the consultant recognised her as a Munchausen patient that she was exposed. I never knew and none of the Resus team had known, as she was so good. Munchausen sufferers crave attention, care and the sympathy generated in a hospital setting.

3. Help an elderly lady cross the Kings Road in Chelsea.

4. Assist a lady in her eighties to put on her bra at 3 a.m. (given as an assist) to help patient to toilet.

5. Feeling funny after smoking a joint.

6. Cuts to hands. There were lots of these, the worst being a 6ft 6in rugby player with a paper cut to his pinkie.

7. Toilet brush and other items stuck in various parts of people's bodies – a toilet brush, was one of the funniest I attended.

8. Young people feeling unwell: hundreds of calls.

9. Foreigners abusing the NHS system. Even before entering the country, they believed that they might receive better treatment, with regard to housing and benefits, if they attended a UK hospital. I remember seeing a documentary where migrants were briefed about what to do, and what they could receive, according to what they claim. That's not to say all migrants are like that.

10. Hundreds of people with colds, as well as headache, migraines. It beggars belief.

11. 'I have cancer' calls.   12. Hundreds and hundreds of drunk calls.

13. People who had asleep in the street and passers-

by thinking they were ill or dead.

14. Assisting the elderly to go to the toilet or back to bed.

15. A toe or finger nail coming off.

16. Period pain.

17. Cutting a leg when shaving.

18. Tummy ache.

19. A man's penis caught in zip.

20. Tongue hanging out. When the patient thought we weren't looking they would put it back in their mouth. Try doing this: your tongue will always go back in your mouth. The patient was not ill nor on any medication that might cause this. Chelsea and Westminster Hospital had the pleasure of this idiot.

21. Toothache

The following can be a consequence of sending ambulances to people that do not really require them. I remember a young girl, who had a serious asthma attack. There were no emergency vehicles available. Control kept broadcasting for an available crew. Maybe they were all out of their area; all were busy. An ambulance crew "greened up" meaning they were ready for another call, and they were given the job.

Unfortunately, at that moment, the crew was in a West London hospital and the young girl was in East London. She died when she shouldn't have. She should never have died from an asthma attack.

Weirdo Paedo

Sick, weirdo, paedo,

You bide your time, wait to strike,

You wait for innocents,

With speed, and momentum,

To satisfy, your evil ways.

3. The Alien

There was a guy I sometimes worked with, called David Ian Kinnock. He was a prat: intelligent, yet without common sense. He should never have joined the Ambulance Service; it was too difficult for him. It later transpired that he had joined for the wrong reasons.

He was an alcoholic. He took pills to wake up, and pills to go to sleep. He drank enough coffee to sink a battleship. He was about 5ft 6ins tall, well covered around the middle, with a piggy face, a piggy nose and small eyes that were greeny-blue in colour. His skin tone was a pale, sickly pink, tinged with grey, I thought he was an alien, it was because of the way he walked: he would take a step forward, and his upper body would be two steps behind. He spoke with a lisp, and a bit of a hiss.

Without fail he would come to work with bits of loo paper stuck on him where he cut his face shaving, he was covered in spots of blotted blood. He would go straight to the kitchen and make himself a cup of coffee and drink it while he smoked a fag. He would do this three times. It was his ritual: he never spoke to anyone until he had his three coffees and fags. He stank.

He would eventually grunt a 'hello', then go straight into a coughing fit. He was painful to watch, as well as to listen to. He had unusually small hands and feet. He had close cropped, sandy-coloured hair. He was about 40 years old, and although academically intelligent, he was greedy, selfish and very opinionated. And he had to have the last word. I often asked myself, why did I have to work with him?

Although we all wore the same uniform, he never looked smart. He had a smell that emanated from him: it wasn't just the fags and the alcohol, it was something else. That smell made its way into your body making you sick. I gagged if he sat next to me. I felt sorry for the patients – and I had to work with him.

I swear he was an alien lizard.

He could never sit still, always itching for a job, yet useless when he got one, although everyone else enjoyed the odd quiet spell. He was a crap driver, a crap medic and an even worse navigator. We didn't have satnavs back then, so we all had to read maps, but he couldn't.

On this particular day it was so quiet we decided to engage him in conversation, to make him open up to us, learn something about him – like what planet he came from. Stuff like that.

He started reminiscing about his life in South Africa, where he had been a teacher. There were no females on station that day. He said he was an English teacher in a private school. He told us that during the summer holidays he had remained at the boarding school, to look after the girls who never went home, or didn't go on holiday with their parents.

He was the only teacher; part of a skeleton staff. He looked after young girls aged from 10 to 15 years.

We listened intently, not wanting him to clam up. So we egged him on: we knew where this was going. Everyone that had previously worked with him knew he was odd in a perverted way. He was finally comfortable enough with us, to open up. He said he had to look after about fifteen girls. He said he would order pizza and other takeaway snacks, as well as some vodka and orange juice. He told the girls they could come and watch a horror film in his quarters.

When the girls got scared, he told them to get in his bed, so he could look after them.

He gave them orange juice with a shot of vodka to 'loosen' the girls up. He said he'd had eight girls in his bed one night. He said he "consoled" them.

Suddenly he began to clam up. He must have seen a look in someone's eye, and read it like words, falling to the floor: 'You're a fucking p

    a

       e

         d o

            p h

               i l e.'

He stopped and went to make coffee. The phone rang and two crews went out. I was alone with the alien.

He used to give us lots of unintentional laughs. On one job we went to, a chap who had fallen up a few steps and cracked his skull. He was bleeding quite profusely. The alien never wore any gloves, despite all the blood, he took twenty minutes to dress a wound. He ended up covered in the patient's blood. He kept wiping his face as he was sweating so much. He spread the bloke's blood all over himself, so that in the end it looked as if I was taking two patients to hospital.

When he finally sat the patient in the back and took a history, the bloke told him he was HIV Positive I laughed at him for having smeared infected blood all over himself. He never understood that if infected blood got into his eye, he could become infected

Another time a ninety-year-old lady, who was extremely frail, had fallen out of bed after her home help had left on a Friday night. The heating was on high and she fell between the bed and a long radiator. She must have screamed in pain all Friday and Saturday, and by Sunday she had full thickness burns along one side of whole body. She no longer felt pain.

Two carers arrived on Monday morning and we got a call at 8 a.m., to assist an elderly lady back to bed, after she had fallen out of bed. So much for the carers! They never looked at her, never spoke to her.

We saw the full thickness burns immediately, placed her on our stretcher, and I drove while the alien put a cannula into her arm, to give her some fluids. I put in a Blue Call to St George's in Tooting. She was in a bad way. We got there in five minutes.

As I jumped out of the vehicle I was met by Amelia, the strictest of nursing sisters, who was very old school. I liked her. We got on. But she took no prisoners. I opened the back doors to find the alien jumping up and down, screaming at the top of his voice: 'She's bleeding. She's bleeding.' He screamed this four times.

The sister looked at me and I looked back, trying not to laugh. I gave her a look of understanding. He hadn't put the cannula in properly which was why she was bleeding. But that was the least of her worries. Gladys was not long for this world and died soon after.

And the alien remained a prat.

Another time we had a woman of 60 years who had had a heart attack. Again, he could not get a cannula into her arm. Most of us on station practised on each other or on ourselves, as it was important.

He started resus in the back of the ambulance, while I put in a Blue Call to St George's. The lady was still unconscious, but I got us there in five minutes. The alien was in a sweat. I parked up at St George's to find the same strict sister waiting for us.

As before, I jumped out, opened the back doors and pulled at the stretcher. To everyone's horror the stretcher fell to the floor. He had his foot on the release catch, instead of waiting for me to release the legs of the stretcher first. The patient fell from the stretcher to the floor, bouncing up and down several times, as she had crashed to the floor from over 3 feet. But something miraculous happened to our patient: she opened her eyes and saw a dozen people staring at her, but didn't realise what had happened.

The sister looked at me, and I just smiled back at her. At least it was a good outcome, and the patient lived for many years afterwards.

One summer we were called to a job in Wandsworth Road, at a small block of flats. A ten-year-old girl had experienced a severe asthma attack. Her grandmother

was looking after four children during the school summer holidays and was waiting outside for us. It was a very hot and humid day, with lots of pollution hanging in the air, caused by lots of buses and lorries doing what they did best – polluting.

I opened up the back doors, just as the youngest kid ran off. The grandmother went after him with the other two kids. The alien sat the girl in the back, and took a history. Then he gave the child oxygen but no Ventolin. I told him I was going to look for the others. I walked to a junction and peered around the corner, where I saw the grandmother and the other kids, I waved to her to hurry up, then walked back to the ambulance.

As I approached, I noticed the back doors were shut. Why would anyone shut them in that heat? He had also pulled down the blinds.

I had been watching him like a hawk, as had everyone who worked with him. Had I just slipped up? I walked quickly to the back doors, and opened them up quickly and quietly.

The young girl was naked. I shouted at him, 'What the fuck are you doing?' There were protocols to follow, not only for the

patient's safety, but for our own. He had his fat, sweaty, piggy alien hand on her little chest; the other hand held a stethoscope as he pretended to listen to her breathing. I wanted to beat him up there and then, even if it meant kicking the crap out of him in front of the kid. But I never.

He dressed the girl before her grandmother got back. I felt sick. I intended to deal with this alien. The grandmother turned up and I got them all settled, before I drove to St Thomas's, by the river.

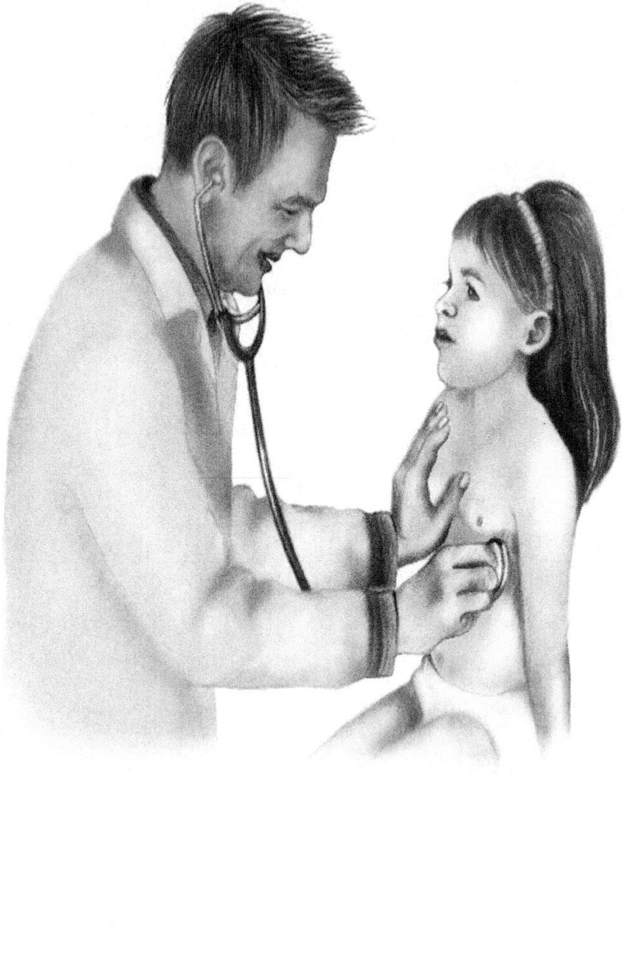

After he booked the child in, I gave him so much abuse. Any normal person would have hit back at me, either verbally or physically. I was praying for him to hit me. Then I could have him, fucking alien.

We never spoke anymore after that, but I made sure I told everyone on station. Word travelled quickly, and he put in for a transfer almost immediately. But I wasn't finished with him. I reported him to my superiors and later told the police. My superiors didn't want to know: one of them said, 'Don't tell me, I don't want to know'. That's how good our management was.

The alien left Lavender Hill, and became a first responder which meant that he could attend calls on his own, before anyone else arrived.

Idiots, all of them! I should have spoken to the grandmother and the hospital staff and made it official at the time. But now it was too late to correct my mistake.

One day the alien would get caught. As for the management ...

Lord

You knocked on my door,

You wanted sex,

A powerful man,

A lord,

A creep,

A beater of women,

An abuser of power,

You knocked on my door, Every week,

You wanted my sex,

You dressed in heels,

You made me kneel,

You had your way,

And wouldn't pay.

You beat me

Till I bled.

4. Lord

I often took overtime at the main ambulance station of Wimbledon Hill. It was far quieter than Lavender Hill and it made a nice pleasant change to work there.

I was working with a newbie, who had been posted to this station as a relief. She'd done her training at Highgate Hill, which was a main station as well as a training school.

She was about 5ft 5 ins tall, with long black hair and blue eyes, she was a lovely lady, good looking, and great to talk to; she had great smile and good conversation. I liked her, she was easy to chat to. She also laughed easily, which made me feel comfortable. I like to hear people, laugh. There wasn't nearly enough laughter in the world, especially by me.

Her name was Jane. She came from southern Ireland. She had come to train in London, with the intention of returning home. She had an accent, but it wasn't harsh; it had a nice mellow sound to it, maybe because she was half-Greek.

We were down to work a late shift: 1500–2300. I thought how easy this shift would be: a real walk in the park at this quieter station.

We had a few calls which amounted to a few belly aches, period pain, a headache, and an 'unwell'. But when Jane asked the unwell patient in what way he was unwell, he could not say. She took all his observations and everything seemed fine. He had no history of illness, no pain, his blood pressure was normal, as was the ECG.

But he wanted to go to hospital, so we took him.

We returned to station after that exciting job. I put the kettle on, and asked Jane if she wanted a drink. We sat on station for 20 minutes drinking our tea and watching TV. Then the phone rang.

Jane took details as I went to open the garage doors.

The call was given as: 30-year-old female; facial and body cuts; bleeding profusely. Jane noted the address, times and initials. The location was only a few minutes away.

Jane climbed aboard. I drove quite fast, even though the job was on our doorstep. It could be serious. We arrived in 3 minutes, jumped out and made our way into the house, where the door had been left wide open.

We saw and heard no one. The place was in darkness, although I did notice a dim light on upstairs. We walked into the back room where the kitchen and dining room were, and I switched on lights as we progressed through the house.

There was a lady on the floor whimpering. She had lost a fair bit of blood.

Her name was Rachel. She'd had an argument with a man, who was now hiding upstairs. Jane dressed her injuries – she was in a bad way – while I got a chair and blanket. I decided to call the police as it was clearly an assault.

As I went to call Control, I saw a stream of police vehicles heading towards me: six police cars, one unmarked, and a van. I thought it was odd; a bit of overkill.

It was a scene to behold: eight emergency vehicles, lights flashing, headlights illuminating the road, and the sound of all the sirens. The sound made my ears ring. People were at their windows, looking out, wondering what was going on. I rushed back in to Jane, before the police went in. I was worried about her as the assailant was still in the house.

Rachel had been cut to pieces. She was a prostitute – or a 'public service provider' – working mainly from home. She serviced men and sometimes women. She had had an argument about money with the man, she said. He had a raging temper and had grabbed her hair and smashed her face into the double-glazed patio doors, before pushing her through the opening, which caused more serious cuts.

She was in a bad way, and we needed to get going. We got her onto our chair and wrapped her up, just as the assailant came downstairs.

'Shit!' I said to myself. 'I know him.' He was a lord and a serving MP.

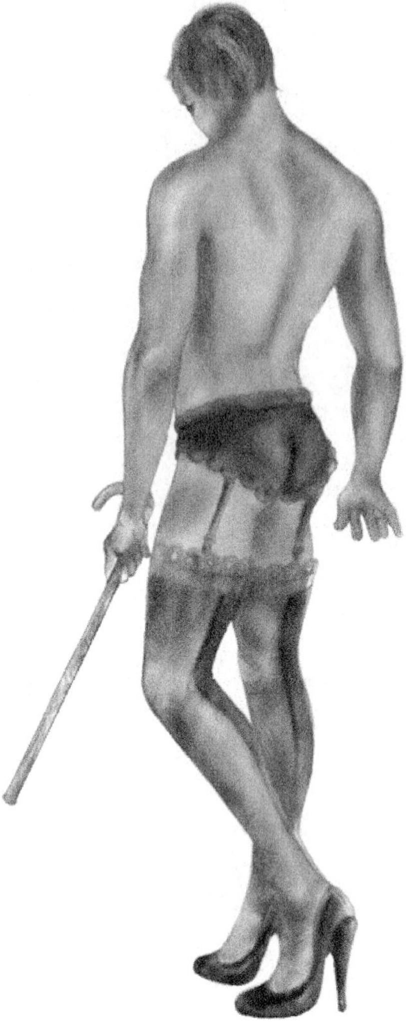

The police threw a sheet over his head so that he would not be recognised by anyone outside. Then they put him in the unmarked car and drove him away. We put Rachel onto our stretcher and gave her fluids and oxygen.

I noticed another cop get into a smart Mercedes and drive off. I began to smell the shitty stench of a cover-up.

A plain clothes officer asked Jane where we were taking Rachel. But before Jane could answer, I said, 'St George's. It's the nearest and she's lost a fair amount of blood'.

He went and spoke to a colleague, then came back. 'Follow me,' he said to Jane, as he looked at me. This stinks.

They told Jane we're going to a private hospital. They didn't care if she lived or died, and probably would have preferred her dead, after all he was an M.P.

Jane answered, 'Okay.' I didn't respond. If Rachel died, the coroner and our employers were going to ask why we never took her to the nearest hospital. We would be in Shit Street, and in serious trouble. We started our journey: two police cars in front of me, lights flashing, sirens blaring. Five police cars and an ambulance making enough noise to wake the dead. I laughed to myself at the absurdity of it all.

I thought quickly about what would, or could, they do if I turned off, and took the patient to the nearest hospital. We couldn't get into trouble, not if we did what was best for the patient. What could the police do to me? Nothing, was my answer.

They could not afford for me to go public, and talk about the man, who had seriously

injured this lady. I was not under their jurisdiction. I told Jane what I was going to do and she agreed. Fifteen minutes had already passed and we were both worried about Rachel.

My chance was coming up – a nice wide turning on the right, and St George's was only 3 minutes away from there. I moved the ambulance, so I could swing right.

The police car in front of me realised what I was about to do, and quickly slowed down and blocked my path. I had no choice: I was unwilling to follow them, but I had no option.

Twelve minutes later, we arrived at a private hospital. It was funny how they were expecting Rachel: they knew all her details, every last thing about her ... and probably about us too. We grabbed a coffee and sat in the ambulance while Jane filled out her paperwork. I jumped in the back, disinfected the stretcher and washed away the sticky blood.

I went back and sat behind the steering wheel. We were now miles out of our own area. If we acquired a job when we were there, we would be off late as we could end up in North London. Jane was just about to call up green to let them know we were ready for our next job. when a policeman rapped on her window. The other police cars had now left.

Jane opened the window and the unshaven cop asked Jane if she had all the paperwork for the job we had just done. Jane replied that she did. He threw me a dirty look as he grabbed all of Jane's paperwork. Then he got into the police car and left.

Jane stared at me. I stared back, thinking, I know

you're shocked, but you never realised who the assailant was.

I told her she ought to call Control to let them know where we were, and what had happened. She did, but before our Control answered her, I knew what was coming.

'What job?' Control said. 'Return to base.'

The cover-up was complete: no paperwork; no names; nothing to prove what we had done, who had been assaulted, and by whom, or even where we had taken our invisible patient.

Jane looked at me in disbelief, I said to her, 'What did you expect? He's a Lord, and a serving MP, with a prostitute. It's been hushed up.'

It wasn't the first time an ambulance crew had attended incidents where wealthy members of the Establishment – including High Court judges, magistrates, barristers and consultants – had beaten their partners. After all, they were human too, prone to the same addictions and feelings as the rest of us.

I wasn't surprised by much anymore. We saw it all in our job. I think I had just expected more from the police, but this proved that there was one law for the Establishment, and one for the rest of us.

It was now 21:30. We had another hour and a half until we finished our shift. By the time we got to Chelsea Embankment we had been given another job.

Jane took the call: female; baby; 10 months old; stuck

in a hoover. Address and times were given, and initials exchanged.

I wanted to laugh. I didn't know what to make of this. It had to be a hoax call. Either way, I drove fast, so that at least we stood a chance of getting into our own area.

Who would believe us getting a job from The Embankment to Mitcham in Surrey, I wondered if we were being punished. Surely there was a vehicle closer than us. I drove fast, on the wrong side of the road, blinding other cars into submission, or forcing them to top and make way ... for a baby ... stuck in a vacuum cleaner.

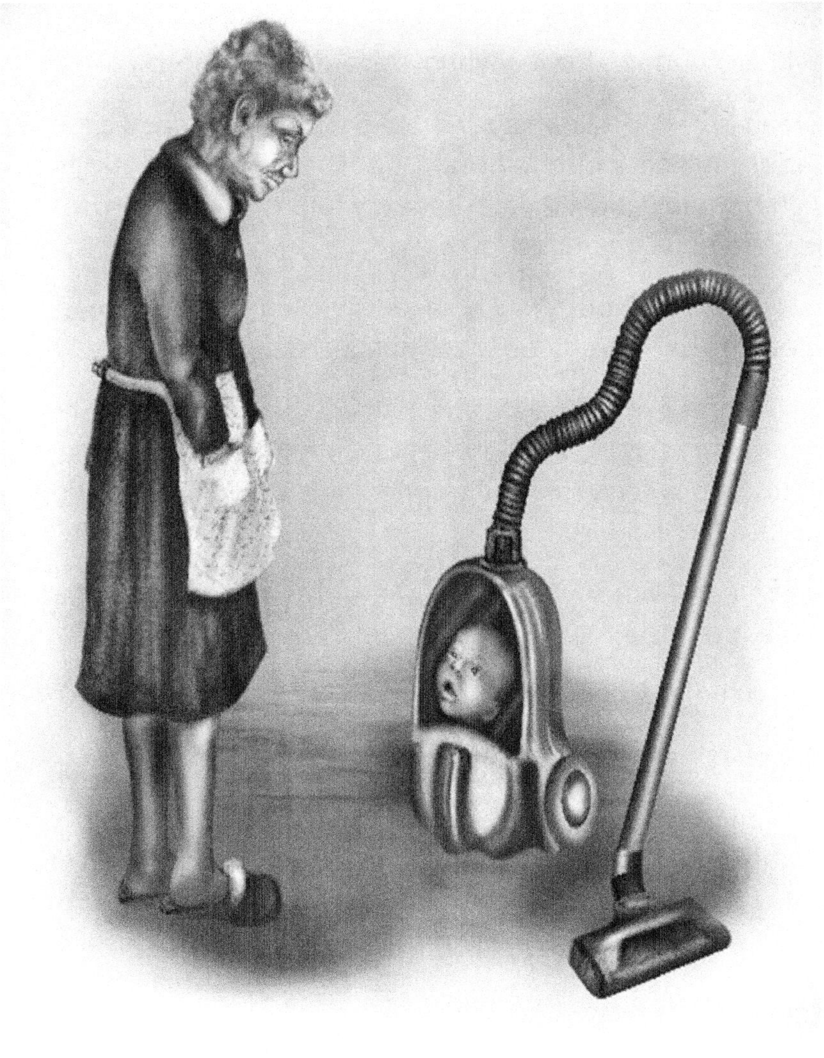

We found out a week later that Rachel lived despite all her serious injuries. We heard nothing from anybody regarding that job.

The siren screamed as I drove, mainly on two wheels. I copped a look at Jane. She had shrunk back into her seat, almost disappearing into her chair. Her skin suddenly looked pale. I put my foot down and drove faster as we were now in familiar territory.

Jane said nothing throughout the whole journey, her voice lost in my speed. We got to Mitcham at 21:55. We needed to find number 21.

Jane spotted a woman in her early fifties outside her front door. She had stringy dark brown hair, with lots of grey in it. She had brown eyes, was unhealthily skinny, and smelt of alcohol. Jane asked her questions, as she led us into the living room.

I kept my back to the wall. I didn't see a baby, only a vacuum cleaner. There was no baby in the room.

Jane then asked the most important question: 'Where is the baby?'

The lady answered, 'In the hoover.' It was a hoover that rolled along the floor.

Jane looked at me. I don't think she'd had much experience of dealing with psychiatric patients. She stared at me, lost for words, so I took the lead and asked Mary if she would like us to take her baby to hospital.

She replied quite sternly, and in a loud voice, 'Why do you think I called you? My baby is in the hoover.'

I said, 'That's fine, Mary. Can you still hear your baby? 'Yes,' she replied.

I told her to grab a coat, her bag and her keys, then I

took the hoover out to the ambulance. Mary insisted I put the hoover on the stretcher. So I did, and left Jane to chat with her. I wasn't looking forward to wheeling the stretcher into A&E in front of our colleagues and nursing staff. When we got to St George's and that's exactly what I did: in order to keep Mary calm, I wheeled the stretcher in, much to everyone's amusement.

Jane told me that when Mary had got pregnant years ago, her husband had decided to leave her, using her pregnancy as an excuse. Her baby had died at 3 months old, from Sudden Infant Death Syndrome (SIDS), as she was 'hoovering' her front-room carpet.

The association was born and it had stuck: she had obviously never got over the death.

Our shift finished exactly at 23:00. When Jane called Control, they asked Jane if we were willing to work on for a couple of hours. We looked at each other, laughed out loud and said 'No thanks'. We left.

VACUUM.

Baby, where have you gone?

Has my OCD swallowed you up

While cleaning carpet?

My baby, where have you gone?

You lost, in my vacuum,

Me lost, in a lifetime's moment.

Naomi

Girl, with the long hair,

Lost, in a moment of time,

Lost in confusion,

Unknowingly, pushed aside,

Fused in time

Locked in death's dark veil.

5. Naomi

Monday July 5th 1999, at 7 am, on a sunny day my partner and I received a call to investigate. The police had been notified as well. The road was very close to our station; it was so close we could have walked it in two minutes.

We arrived well before the police, a woman was standing outside the front door, trying to push it open. I told her to let me have a go, while my partner clamed her down, and tried to get some information.

I pushed at the door, and pushed even harder, but there was something behind the door, stopping it from fully opening. I managed to get half my body inside the hallway.

The following is what we saw, written in the format of a poem.

Naomi

Black ... like white, White ... like black,

You ... like me,

Me ... like you,

Beautiful child,

   Angelic face, covered in a see-through shroud of

sorrow,

Life stolen ... alone,

  In the shadows of darkness,

  Forever six years old,

You were not to blame,

Mother black,

Father white.

Profound and round

  Arguments abound,

and travel round,

 And round,

You, In the middle of an earthquake,

Ripped apart,

Mother cracking at the seams,

 Breakdown, on the horizon,

Into a cavern you fall,

no, way, out,

Father, unable to cope,

  Leaves ... with no hope,

    Neither loses face ... In this fast race,

 Both have lost the pace,

Unable to show ... their face,

Unable to cope,

  Only solution ... dope.

  Take Naomi shopping,

  New pyjamas bought,

Treats all day,

  With lots of play,

  Favourite dinner, and chips,

Chocolates and ice cream and chips,

Bath before bed,

belly full,

Hair brushed, and feeling great,

  Off to bed ... Get up late,

Medicine with a drink,

100 aspirins to take,

Then begin to shake,

A kiss goodnight ... before the fight.

We arrive, and begin our fight,

Door blocked,

we push ... and push, and push,

And slowly ...

creep in,

Mother behind the door,

Tights around her neck,

Held up ...off the floor,

Too late to help,

I look for the next of kin,

Naomi found ...

with Froth on her mouth,

Sister arrives

and Can't believe her eyes

... Just cries, And cries, And cries.

A tragic relationship, where two people could not resolve their differences, escalated to the detriment of the child and ultimately to her death.

The Witness

She took a step

Onto moving stairs

 Her body moved Effortlessly

Taking her to her destiny

 Lower level reached

She faced a decision

Bakerloo or Northern, Northern or Bakerloo?

 Northern chosen

She walked

  She looked immaculate

Perfect,

Black hair

Dark brown eyes

Almost black, and mirrored

Hair in a bun Make-up, perfect

Ruby-red lips

Teeth reflecting light

In this dismal space,

Legs wrapped in a modest skirt

And a top which belied her beautiful Figure.

She was the epitome of beauty

A slow-moving goddess.

She walked 40ft towards the end of The platform

Sat down

Never looking around

Lost in her deliberate thoughts

Her elegant fingers Pulled out a gold cigarette,

And lit it

Passengers looking on And looking ...

Nothing said

She looked at the arrival board

Three minutes of smoking left

The rush of air Signalled the train's arrival

She stood up

Made her way to the edge of life

The speeding train Beckoning her,

Calling her name,

Almost taunting her

To end her life.

She looked at the driver

He looked into her beautiful eyes

And knew

What she was to do

He hit the brakes

Before she jumped

It made no difference

As their eyes met.

she died ...

he screamed ...

I looked on ...

The above poem was written with the benefit of information from witnesses and information at the coroner's court, as well as my own perception.

6. Tracks of my Tears

I hated night shifts, and I hated the next day even more. I always felt fucked, tired, with a lack of energy after lack of sleep, stomach playing up, and eating crap. It continued like that until my nightshifts finished.

At night, the jobs we did tended to be a bit more serious, but that wasn't always true.

There were day shifts, when you went to really serious jobs that were unmatched by night jobs, which tended to be more assaults or alcohol-related.

I was on a nightshift with a relief. We were returning from St Thomas's, and were in Wandsworth Road when we got a call to go to Clapham Junction Train Station.

It was for a male, hit by train, platform 11. NFD.

We pulled up outside. It was about 3 a.m. We got our gear and ran towards the job. We reached the staircase for platform 11 and ran up. I stopped, just for a second, as I heard one of my favourite Bob Dylan songs playing in the distance. We were going to a macabre job and there was poetry wafting in the air; a magical clarity to it, like when you hear buskers in the Underground singing

– it always sounded good, almost angelic. Dylan always sounded good.

I heard Dylan's words wafting gently towards us, (the relief I was working with had no idea about music). I could hear the second chorus of "its all over now baby blue"'

I got to the top and saw my partner standing in blood and brains. I shouted at him to look at his feet. He lifted his left foot and looked down at his boot. As he lifted his foot, the blood and brain matter clung to his boot, causing strands to stick to his boot and the platform. When he saw what he was standing in, he jumped up and somehow twisted away from the goo. But I could see the horror in his eyes. The song continued:

the last verse of "its all over now baby blue, for some reason I thought it fitting.

We saw the station staff and we knew we were too late. All I could hear in my head was 'It's all over now, Baby Blue'.

I looked over to my right. There was a fella in his twenties crying, hysterical. The Old Bill turned up, as well as the Transport Police.

The two friends had just returned from holiday in Spain. They were both drunk, waiting for a train to take them home to Brighton. One threw the other's luggage onto the tracks. He jumped down to retrieve it, and was screamed at by a guard to get off the tracks, as an engine was coming towards the station, fast.

His mate ran to the edge of the platform to try lift him out, but he couldn't. His friend was a dead weight, and he couldn't pull him up. There was no one around

to help him, the station was deserted, apart from the guard who was on the other platform. He said, he'd had his friend's hands, but had to let go just as the engine struck. His friend died instantly, his staring face forever imprinted on his mind forever. How quickly he sobered up. Thank the stars, we never had to go and pick up the pieces. It used to be our job, but now transport police do this.

'Desolation Row' had now started to play; another Dylan song. I made the young fella come with us to hospital. He wasn't in a fit state for anything else. There was nothing we could say to him. He was accompanied by the police. How does someone live with that? I could foresee lots of problems for him. He was never going to get over

it – never.

I, along with some of my crew-mates, had been under trains several times. It was part of the job, but it was still very unnerving.

I would constantly ask myself: Did they turn the power off? Will the power stay off? These thoughts were constantly going through my mind. Had one shift finished, and another one started? Were there staff who might not know what was going on?

It was always a long and difficult job to assist someone, who had been hit by a train. I remember a psychiatric patient once. We were going to St George's with a patient, and we

could see HEMS (the Helicopter Emergency Medical Service) circling above Tooting Broadway Station, like a big red buzzard waiting to pounce and carry out its mission.

We got to St George's, booked in and got a coffee. We drank and listened to some sounds. I greened up and immediately got another job to Wimbledon Park.

The Wimbledon Park job was to platform 1: female, suicide attempt, still under train.

NFD.

No sooner had the call finished, than I could see the station, we'd got there in a flash. I and my partner Eric took everything we needed. We were told the power was off, but

nevertheless, we asked again before making our way under the train. We could hear the helicopter circling above us and I was grateful that a doctor would be present, if needed.

We crawled under the train. Fuck! I don't think I could do that now! She was alive; moaning and writhing in pain, but pretty much intact,

He left arm was fucked, still connected by sinew and some blood vessels; bones were cracked; head cracked. She was in a bad way: her stomach was distended; she had a bad head injury and internal bleeding. We were amazed that she was still breathing.

Somehow her left arm was trapped under some timber, we tried to free her arm, when we heard some idiot say 'Hurry up' to us. We looked at each other and towards the platform, where we saw the familiar orange jumpsuits of hems. We knew the doctor would not say 'Hurry up!' to us, so it had to be the idiot paramedic.

In unison we shouted, 'Shut the fuck up, you prat!'

We had silence now. We freed her arm, and got the scoop under her. It was bloody difficult working under a train. All our movements were restricted. The police told us they were going to move the train over us and away, so that we could remove our patient. We had to make sure to hold her down, restrict her movements, or we could all be toast.

That was fucking scary! We both got as low as we could, kissing the ground.

The train moved away from us and we finally got her up, and off the tracks and into our ambulance. The doctor gave her some pain relief. The HEMS medic never said a word to either of us. We made our way to St George's, where the police officer told us that she had tried to jump at Tooting Broadway Underground station 40 minutes earlier.

So, it had been the same person, which meant that the HEMS vultures had got its

prey.

She went into Resus, and then into intensive care. We saw one of the nurses two days

later, who told us she had died, which wasn't a surprise. But then she said, 'You won't believe this. Guess who the driver of the train was?'

We both said we didn't know. 'Her son,' she said.

Who would have believed that? But it was true. She hadn't known her son would be driving the train, at that time, on that day. Her son thought she was still an inpatient at Springfield Psychiatric Hospital.

What were the chances of that happening?

I have been to many 'one-unders'. The first one was while I was training. It was at Camden Town; a male jumper who died. All those I have attended have never survived. People had to be very desperate and have no doubts in their mind about wanting to end it all. They only had one chance to do it right; to end it all, or they could find themselves in a hospital bed, spoon- or drip- fed ... forever.

Krazy Killer

You made me do this,

It wasn't me, idiot,

It was you, not me,

I saw you stab that lady,

Don't blame me, fool.

You did it!

7. Krazy Killer

The day was warm, the sun was shining, people were smiling. It's funny how people are much nicer and happier on a sunny day. And it was a nice day; a gorgeous day; too nice for work.

I remember my crew-mate and I were both wearing short-sleeved shirts, as we sat outside with the other crews, waiting for a job. We were sunbathing and chatting, drinking long, cold drinks, and chilling out.

The phone rang. My mate went to answer it, then rushed back downstairs.

We had a thirty-something female, stabbed multiple times. The call was in Balham at a halfway house, for people with addictions, and some mentally ill patients. They were all at different stages of recovery.

We knew it well. I drove.

We arrived at a totally surreal scene; a scene from an American movie, except that this was real and we were in the movie.

I pulled up. Police with riot shields lined our path, tension and anxiety on all their faces. I tried not to look at the police, as they were a very menacing presence, with their riot shields and their guns, and clubs.

We were shouted at, screamed at by the police, told where to go. Everyone's adrenaline was through the roof, and I could feel mine going that way. No one has control of their adrenaline release, that's why all the police, present in the building were all hyper, it was the incident. It must have been bad.

We were told the patient was at the end of a corridor and the assailant was still in the building.

We rushed to our patient – a female social worker. Blood on the floor. Blood everywhere. She 'looked dead'.

I touched her skin. She felt waxy, a bad sign.

We got her onto the trolley. No time to waste. We had to move. We pushed our way through the arch of shields.

Police smashed down a door somewhere upstairs. Shouting and screaming, with crashing of doors.

We loaded up. A female police officer joined us in the ambulance. We did a quick survey of the patient. She had

multiple stab wounds.

It turned out that she had been interviewing this chap all alone, in an office or his room. As she spoke to him, he turned and pulled out a nine-inch knife.

She lurched back, ran for the door, her back to him. He stabbed her twice.

She turned to fight him off. She had defensive wounds to her hands and arms, she opened the door, and ran. He stabbed her again, She turned to fight. More defensive wounds. He lunged at her and stabbed her in the stomach. She

fell to the ground. He sat on her, around her waist, pulled out another knife and stabbed with one hand, then the other. Again and again. Over and over again.

He stabbed and stabbed and stabbed in a frenzy.

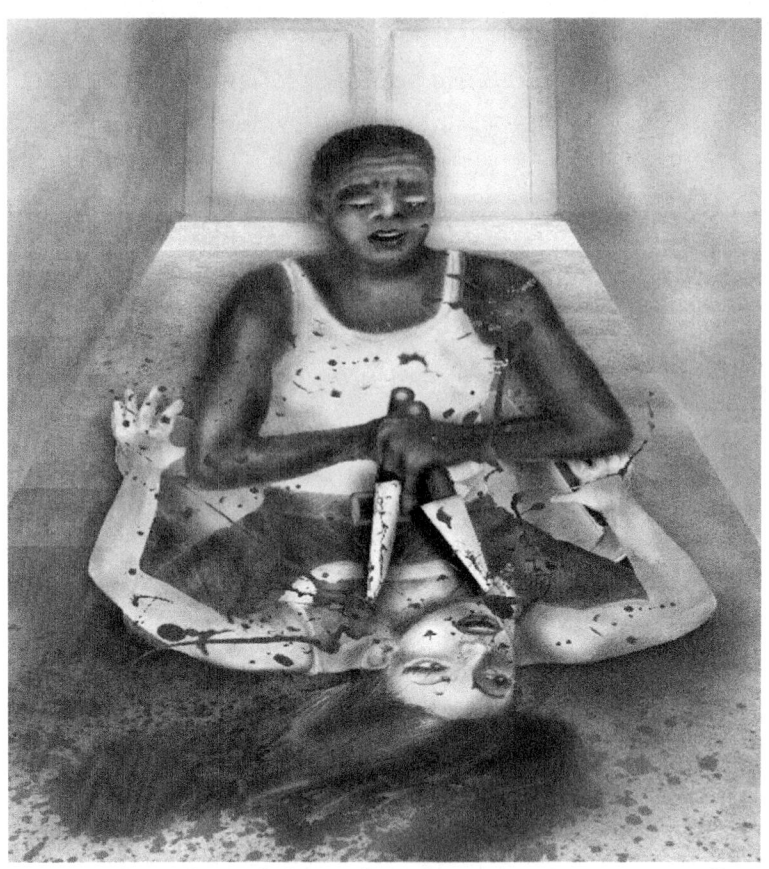

He must have heard the police sirens, so he ran up a flight of stairs and hid, locked himself away, secluded. Our patient intubated, I ran to the front, started up the engine and drove. Time was of the utmost

importance. She was in a bad way: depleted of fluid, dead by all

accounts, but we had to try. She had too many puncture wounds.

The body is like a plumbing job – a closed system: if there are burst pipes in the heating system, it won't work properly. It can't afford any leaks in order to function properly.

We saw at least twenty stab wounds, her bare body, and full of holes, blood weeping out in tune with chest compressions.

My mate and the policewoman were covered in her blood, as was I. I drove steadily, but fast; as fast as I could.

My Control bleeped me. I didn't answer. They called me again. I replied.

'W121,' they said. 'We are ordering you to stop by the Common, and await HEMS (the air ambulance).'

My mate and I both heard, but I wasn't going to stop. Didn't they fucking know me yet? We were ultimately responsible for our patient.

I picked up the mic and told them to 'Fuck right off!' then threw the mic at the windscreen. It bounced back and hit me on the face, causing me to curse them again.

I believed I knew their game: HEMS had decided that this would be good publicity. I believed they cared more about their image than the patient; it wasn't their first priority.

Funding was their game, their image, and of course free publicity. Why else would they tell me to stop when I am 2 minutes from a trauma centre. It would have made great news,

how they cut open a social worker, north to south, east to west, gave open-heart massage at the roadside; how they tried their best, but unfortunately failed in their attempt to save her life. Most of my colleagues felt the same way.

Well I didn't play games like that. I cared: patient first. Always first. I knew she was going to die, but I still wasn't playing games.

I drove and in two and half minutes we were there. If we'd waited for the helicopter it could have taken another twenty minutes.

Jobs like this needed many hands, including a doctor, and the best place for that was a hospital.

We pushed her into Resus. I was stressed, really stressed. Adrenaline kicked right in; I could have fought a herd

of elephants, never mind the wankers in Control. I wanted to be on my own. I was too shocked to

even cry. I needed to calm down. I set about cleaning the ambulance, thinking of her; a

social worker; a nice woman. There was blood everywhere, I remember her well. I still remember her name, and

will never forget it. My mate brought me a hot black coffee and helped me clear up.

After 10 minutes the police joined us. The Resus team had called it. There was no blood left in her body – exsanguination of the body; total blood loss; all fluid gone.

We gave the police our details, for the Coroner's Court if required.

The assailant was arrested: a mentally ill patient who had probably not taken his medication.

Whose fault was this?

In my book it was the Government's fault for closing psychiatric hospitals, where people were watched, and given their daily dose of medication at regular times.

Our patient wasn't the first in the Tooting area; others were injured in similar incidents? After all we had a psychiatric hospital nearby. Sometimes when you walked around these hospitals you never knew who was a psychiatric patient, and who was normal, if you can call anyone normal anymore. Staff at St Georges had been assaulted and stabbed on several occasions, and had to be taken to A & E, by ambulance, stationed at St George's hospital.

We were not required at the coroner's court.

After the post mortem we found out she had been stabbed 127 times.

I thought a plumber couldn't deal with that many leaks ... nor can a doctor.

Dead Before One

A glorious day,

I'm filled with love and joy,

I have a baby boy,

Something hit my door,

I swore,

Death came knocking and took him.

Young and happy,

A beautiful day,

Sunshine, and a deep blue sky,

Wind gone, before yesterday,

Early morning dew,

Quenching the thirst of flowers,

Me dancing ...

On a cloud,

Puffy, like stretched-out cotton wool,

I tippy-toe, and jump with joy,

I'm proud ... Still round,

Gave birth to nine-pound baby boy,

God, I'm filled with joy.

Baby Jack,

In the sack,

He comes with me,

While I do chores,

One bed made, two made,

Jack smiling,

Wind, I thought,

Makes us fraught,

Jack still smiling,

I visit the loo.

I scream out,

Mum! Jack ...Jack ... Jack.

Please smile ... Jack ... Jack.

Call an ambulance,

I scream, with anguish,

Help meeeeeeeeeeeeeeeeeeeeeeeeeeeeeeeeeeeeeeeeee,

Please, help,

I rush downstairs,

Mum and I crying,

screaming,

Not knowing what to do,

We wait,

by the door,

On the floor,

legs not working.

Arms flailing, screams filling air

We get the call,

Our turn to go,

First responder joins us too,

We arrive,

4 minutes gone,

People standing outside,

You know it's genuine,

When you see them

 jump, Up and down,

and pull at their hair,

We run, I shout to my mate,

Turn the ambulance round,

I hold the baby, Gingerly,

Gently,

Mum gets in the back,

Alone in her thoughts,

screaming,

Silently, or so I thought,

Her mum, still on the floor,

Wailing like a banshee,

Our driver shuts us in,

And begins our drive,

Call put in, to Chelsea and West,

Jeff bags the baby,

Pushing air Into tiny lungs,

Looking for a sign,

Mum still screaming,

Her tears streaming,

8 minutes gone,

I do tiny compressions,

Two fingers used,

Looking for a sign,

Mum screaming,

I hear her now,

No sign.

10 minutes gone,

We arrive,

resus in progress,

Handover made,

We wait … and wait,

While the doctors,

and the team do their best,

Mum still screaming,

All alone, with twenty in the room,

I leave Jerry, And walk to Mum,

I throw my arm around her,

She's totally unaware,

We wait … and wait …

But it's tooooo late,

40 minutes gone,

They call it,

Jack, pronounced dead,

It's not fair,

I whispered silently … To my brain,

I look at mum with dread,

I could not look at her,

I let her go and rush to the loo,

I cry ... and cry ...

I wash my face,

eyes red, and tearful,

I grab a coffee with Jeff,

He asks me, Is this your first?

I replied, Shied, and said yes,

My first,

He shook his head,

I asked how many he had ...

T h i r t e e n, he said.

A WOMAN WHOSE HUSBAND DIES IS CALLED _ _ _ _ _ _ _ _ _ _

A MAN WHOSE WIFE DIES IS CALLED _ _ _ _ _ _ _ _ _

A CHILD WHOSE PARENTS DIE, IS CALLED _ _ _ _ _ _ _

A COUPLE WHOSE BABY DIES ARE CALLED ? ? ? ? ?

widow hearts No spoken
words parent
          good-bye
  widower sadness
  ache tears
before   loses
                        still
  farewell   child
              lose you
flow   gone
    still
  orphan,   no word

Patients, Staff, Doctors, and Nurses

All work and no play

Makes Casanova eager

Nurses bored with toast

Seeking carrots with hot love

Patients looking on bemused.

8. Patients, Staff, Doctors, and Nurses

Every ambulance crew and every manned police car all over the country is likely to have at least one job per shift, if not more, that is a total waste of time; a job that's a real pain.

One of my mates from Brixton Hill Ambulance Station had the misfortune to attend a twenty-year-old female, who was shit-faced drunk and possibly on drugs. They arrived and, before they could ask her anything, she demanded to go to St Thomas's. Sometimes it was just easier to take them, than to argue, if you know an argument is coming, so they took her.

She sat in the ambulance, spat on the floor, and leaned back in the chair, then placed her dirty boots on the stretcher. My mate told her several times to take her feet off the stretcher. On the fourth occasion, he used his hand to lift her foot off the bed.

She struck like lightning, pouncing like a cat. She grabbed his hand and bit him as hard as she could. She would not release her bite. Her teeth dug into my mate's left hand, above and below the thumb.

He screamed in pain. He had no choice, other than to start punching her with his free hand. He punched her several times in the face, but she still never let go.

The driver stopped and called for immediate police assistance, then jumped in the back to assist his mate. She eventually let go. She was in a frenzy. The police came, arrested her, and took her away.

They continued to St Thomas's as he needed treatment for his bite. They arrived at the hospital and he was seen by a junior doctor, who cleaned his wound, dressed it and then he was allowed to leave. He filled out a report about the incident and went home.

I saw him a couple of days later. His injury had worsened. The doctor at St Thomas's had made a serious mistake and not prescribed any antibiotics, or even administered a tetanus injection.

My friend showed me his wound. I could see the poison travelling up his arm. He had pain at the elbow and under his armpit. He could have lost his arm. It's incredible what you can become infected with, from a

Human bites can be very serious; they can pass on Hepatitis B and C, herpes, syphilis, tuberculosis and tetanus. It's even possible to get HIV, although this is unlikely.

His hand had swollen and he had lymphangitis, an inflammation of the lymphatic system.

The patient that bit him had lost two teeth from biting him that ferociously. The young lady that bit my friend was successfully prosecuted, and my friend made a full recovery after being off for 3 weeks. Another colleague, who worked in North London,

was called to a phone box in Hendon. They arrived and the driver parked right next to the phone box. The attendant went to the phone box, but never even uttered a word before he was stabbed in the stomach with a syringe full of blood.

He had to wait months to find out if he was clear of all infections. Infected blood that is outside the body for longer than 30 minutes apparently loses its capacity for infection.

We had to learn all aspects of the job quickly: how to read situations quickly, to stop them developing into something serious, or even dangerous. We had to learn to handle drunks, especially younger people, who couldn't handle their booze.

I remember being caught out a couple of times, where the patient vomited in the ambulance. We had to learn quickly. If a drunk patient was accompanied we would give their friends a mop, bucket and gloves, and watch them clean the ambulance.

I never sat too close to any drunk. I would sit and stare at them, looking and waiting for a sign of projectile vomiting.

One time a yuppie prat showed the signs of imminent puking, so I jumped forward, grabbed his thick jumper and pulled it up to his face so he threw up into it. Then I made him hold his jumper like that. He looked a proper idiot walking into A&E like that.

The drunks that wanted conversation were a real pain. What they said never made any sense, if I spoke to them (other than about what was required to do my job) I would say something totally irrelevant so they would not know how to respond. That usually shut them up for the journey.

The psychiatric patients never spoke much, at least not to me. Some had full-blown conversations with themselves. Most would just stare at me. I always sat well away from them, just in case. We never knew what they might have in their pockets. That really was unnerving. Some would fixate on something in the ambulance.

I had more time for them, than the drunks. (Which I'm embarrassed to say, because that's an illness too) They were at least ill, and did not have a choice about it. One psychiatric patient, would be picked

up by one of our crews every week. He was a self- harmer and would stab himself in the stomach, with a large screwdriver regularly. He would be taken to St George's and was known by everyone.

I remember picking up a patient in a street in Wandsworth, next to a building site.

He'd taken a heroin overdose and wasn't breathing. We bagged him, gave him oxygen and a shot of Narcan, an opioid which reverses the effects of heroin.

Within 3 minutes he shot up like a rocket, knowing what we had done to him and his fix. We had spoilt his trip, so he whacked my partner, who was closest, hitting him on the chin. My mate fell backwards, and out of the ambulance.

I called for police assistance. Luckily they were close by and he was made to go to hospital under police escort.

One morning at eight o'clock, JC and I took a patient to St Thomas's: another drunk, not a youngster; one that would rarely puke. We booked him in and managed to get another job not far from St Thomas's, to a disturbance.

A mother had called on behalf of her son. NFD.

We arrived at the block of flats and could hear a commotion inside. The mother opened the door partially and JC stuck his size-11 boot in the doorway, stopping it from closing. He pushed his way in and was confronted with a man running at him with a long bayonet.

JC called to me to get immediate police assistance. I had to run down five flights of stairs, sprint 50 yards to the ambulance and shout 'Zebra zebra! 'into the microphone to control, who would immediately request the police as a matter of urgency. The adrenaline was pumping now and I was keyed up, like a panther waiting to pounce on its prey. That thought was totally crazy, considering my job.

I ran back up to join JC, not knowing what had happened, to find that JC had broken the bayonet in two pieces with his knee, but the patient managed to stab JC in the bollocks with the broken handle end, of the bayonet, before he was subdued. We both held him down. The police arrived within minutes. So, with one PC on each limb and a few to spare, the man was arrested and taken to Lavender Hill Police Station.

The police searched his bedroom before leaving and found he had over thirty weapons hanging on his wall. We gave the police a few details before going to St Thomas's, so that JC could be looked at by a doctor. He wasn't very pleased about dropping his bottoms.

We were stood down for a few hours. JC was lucky: the blade never broke his skin, but he was badly bruised.

We had another drink, and a police officer came and sat with us. We asked what she was here for. She said that a porter who worked there, had had an operation. He had been on a ward, but he had disappeared. No one knew if he'd left the hospital, if he was hiding in the hospital, or even if he'd had been kidnapped.

She asked if we had time to help her search the back- maintenance staircases and levels and we said that we did. It was an enormous hospital and it wasn't a job to give to a lone policewoman, although a search had been carried out earlier.

We searched four of the maintenance levels and found no sign Then we went up to the fifth level and pushed aside the swing doors. JC looked at me and I gave him a knowing look. There was the familiar smell of death; of a rotting corpse. We followed the smell. We were both certain.
I looked at the policewoman. She had never come across this smell before. I had a small jar of Vick with me and I told her to wipe some under her nose.

There he was, still connected to a drip, in his pyjamas, eyes open, with a wry look on his face, lying next to a hot heating pipe. The place was swarming with flies and his rotting body was covered in maggots.

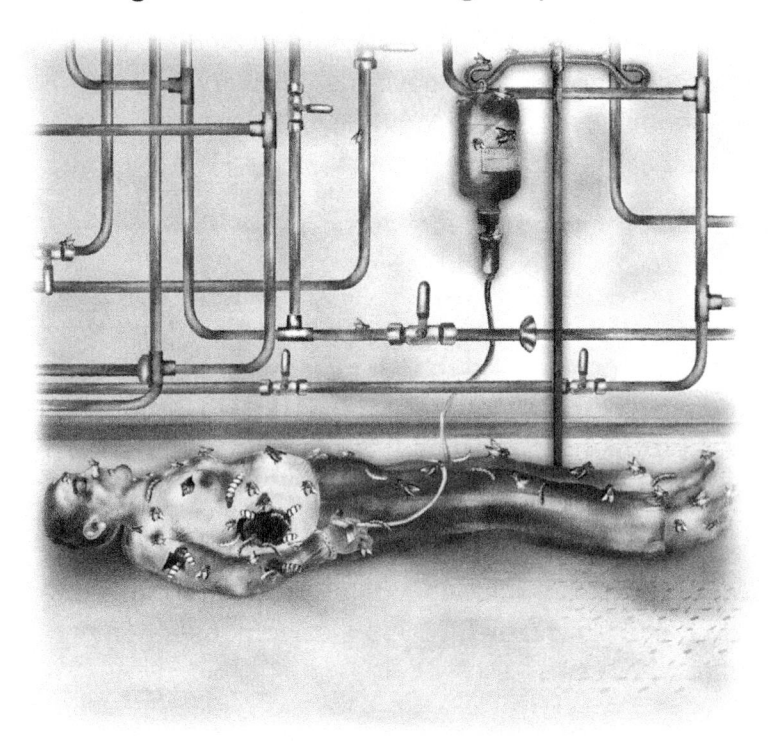

The police woman nearly puked. We made our way out to some of London's comparatively fresh, albeit polluted air, by the river, and asked the police officer how long he had been missing. Three weeks. No one had discovered why he left the ward.

We now had a new type of patient – migrants. They had been briefed by unknown persons in their own countries, to go to hospital with imaginary illnesses and ailments: PTSD, back ache, belly ache, even a headache. I know it sounds racist, and I'm sorry that some may take it as a racist remark. But I wasn't the only person to think like this, a TV company made a documentary about this problem, and even showed one person instructing migrants, in what to do, and how to make successful benefit claims. They even showed jobs that were advertised to migrants before those same jobs were offered to British people.

I'm not saying that all were doing it for that purpose, but many were, and they did not mind telling us either. These individuals had now become a burden on our health service. I remember one patient I went to, who told me in broken English that his tongue would not stay in his mouth. His partner could not speak English.

If I looked at him, his tongue hung down his lip. I made myself understood and found out he had no illnesses, mental or otherwise, and was not on any medication.

That satisfied me: he was taking the piss.

As it was nearing the end of our shift, we decided to take him to Chelsea and West and let them circumnavigate his tongue. At least we would be off on time.

We also had the 'generally unwell' patient, who had no specifics, no symptoms to pass onto the medical staff on arrival at hospital. These people thought that they would be seen quicker if they were brought in by ambulance. Little did they know that they would be sent straight out to the waiting room, for a six- to ten-hour wait.

I chuckled to myself each time – that'd teach 'em.

One summer's day, we had a third man on our ambulance. He had been off sick for some time, so was third-manning with different crews, until he was deemed fit enough to work on his own.

On this particular day we were given a job to Battersea Square, for a man who had collapsed. NFD.

My mate drove us there, but we found no trace of him. I informed Control, who said that they had just received another call to another location, just around the corner.

I spotted him. He was slumped to the floor and something wasn't right. He had a big overcoat on and a huge scarf around his neck.

I jumped out of the ambulance with my toolbox, I recognised him, although I didn't know his name. I had seen him on television many times. I tried speaking to him, but I got no response – he had a blank expression on his face.

I loosened his scarf, and to my horror discovered that

his throat had been slashed, probably with a broken bottle. His clothes under his coat were covered in congealed blood. I called my mate to get the bed out. We were going to have to 'scoop and shoot'; no hanging about. Chelsea and West was only 4 minutes away. We got him in the back and examined him. His injury was horrific: we could look down his throat and see what he had for breakfast. How they had missed his carotid artery, I do not know.

We stabilised him as best we could – this was one job when I needed another pair of hands, and I was grateful for that. I put a blue call in and told Control to inform Chelsea that this patient would require immediate surgery. He had lost a lot of blood and half the oxygen we gave him wasn't getting to his lungs; it was just blowing blood bubbles out of his gaping wound.

We arrived at Chelsea. I handed over and told the senior nurse that he required immediate surgery. She did not believe me, until she took a peek at his wound, when she heaved and ran to the toilet, where she threw up. A consultant took one look at him and immediately sent him for surgery.

The patient lived for a couple of months, then one day he jumped off a high-rise building, killing himself.

We returned to station, after doing three other worthless jobs. We pulled onto station at 18.55 and told control that we were green on station. Control immediately sent us another job via the printer. The phone rang to give us times. I asked my two colleagues to go to the ambulance to listen, to know where other crews were located, and who were available for calls.

I spoke to the controller, who said it was a confirmed cardiac arrest, and I said I would ask the other two if they wanted to work on. They came up and whispered in my ear, as I covered the mouthpiece, then I informed Control that none of us were prepared to work on.

She said, 'Are you refusing an emergency call? A cardiac arrest?'

I said, 'Yes. Are you refusing to send the nearest available ambulance to that emergency?'

'What do you mean?' she asked.

I told her that she had just returned three ambulances from St George's, and that they were the nearest to the cardiac arrest.'

As all calls are recorded, she hung up, and we never heard anymore. They thought that if we had taken this job, then they would still have three ambulances in reserve, but their plan failed.

After a twelve-hour shift, the last thing we wanted was a "suspended", another cardiac arrest. It could have been another two hours before we finished, and there is only so much anyone can do in one day.

I know it may sound harsh but we also have to take into account how safe it is, to keep working on like that?

If we made a mistake after working for twelve hours, who is to blame?

Control never thought of these implications. Maybe if they held back ambulances for real emergencies, the system would work better, instead of their staff burning out.

This is something I could not understand or accept. We were part of the NHS. We played our part in the

health and well-being of our patients, and were trained to a high standard for fieldwork. So why was it that some doctors and nurses did not give us the respect or credit we deserved and demanded. Ninety per cent of the time it was junior doctors and nurses that tried to undermine us in one way or another.

I remember another occasion, where we were given a call to Kings Road, Chelsea, for a road traffic accident. We arrived in 3 minutes, to find two ladies doing CPR. It turned out that the driver of the car had crashed after he had a heart attack and died.

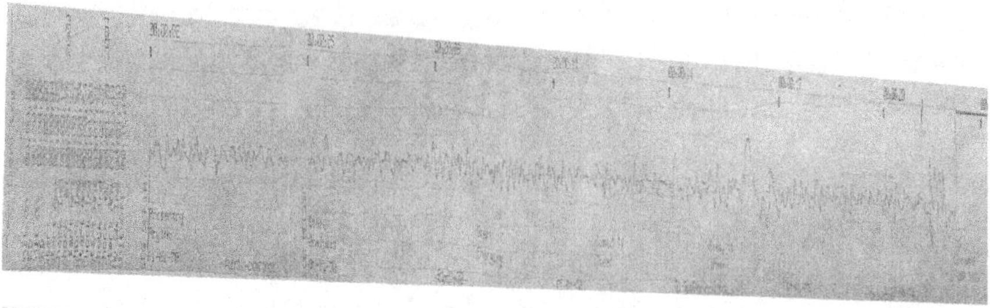

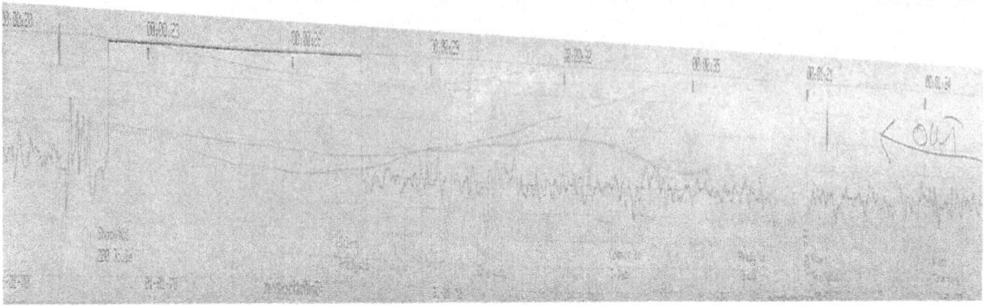
OUT

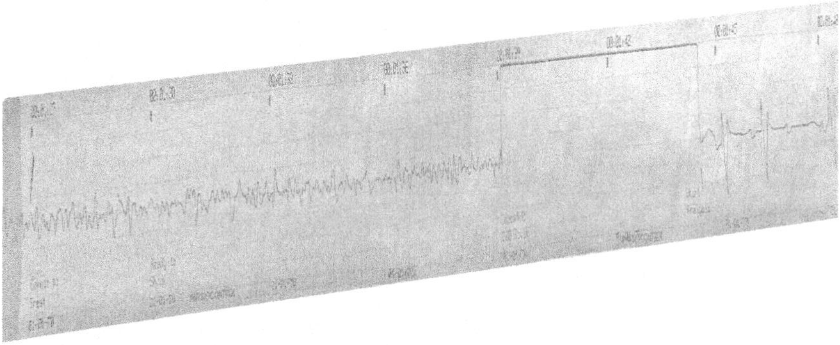

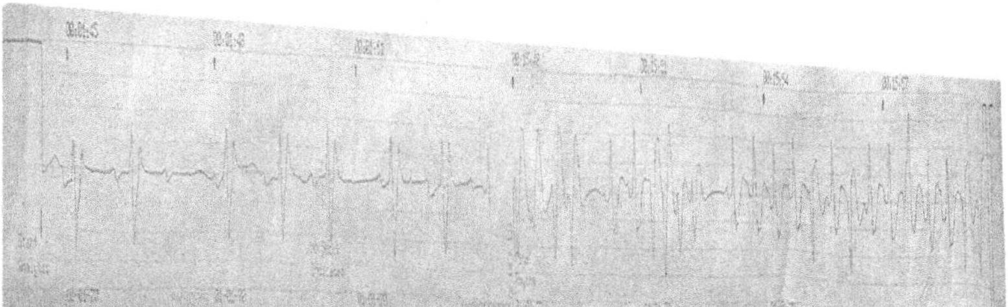

It was a great and lucky day for the German tourist: the two ladies doing CPR were nurses on their lunch break from Chelsea and West. They stayed with us while I wired him up to our defibrillator. His rhythm was in VF; a shockable rhythm.

I zapped him. Nothing. We carried on with CPR. Another shockable rhythm. I zapped him again. He was back in the Land of the Living.

We thanked the nurses and got our patient in the ambulance, along with his wife. My partner put in a blue call to Chelsea and West for a sixty-year-old, conscious, post-cardiac arrest.

Our patient sat up in the ambulance, on the way to the hospital, chatting with me and his wife. This was so rare and the best cardiac arrest I attended, with a great outcome. Now he was sitting bolt upright in Resus, asking about his BMW car. A junior doctor came up to me, and said that we must have made a mistake, about him being in cardiac arrest. I asked him if he thought we could not recognise a dead patient.

He looked at me as if I should not dare to question him.

I went out to the ambulance and printed off a strip from the defibrillator, which showed every action we took, and the inaction of his heart. It showed where our patient had flat-lined, when we got a shockable rhythm, and when we shocked him twice, and when he came back to his normal sinus rhythm.

I took it to the stuck-up prat and made a point of showing it to him and explaining the rhythm strip to him, in a loud voice, so that all his colleagues could hear. Did the doctor really think that we were incapable of doing our job and saving a life?

We were far better qualified to deal with any emergency than any junior doctor was.

That is what we were trained for. I felt a sense of achievement at the doctor's 'Embarrassment', both patient and wife thanked us profusely before we left.

Every workplace has its problem staff, I don't care what anyone thinks, says or does, argue with me if you want, but I could never understand why the ambulance service employed young women who could not lift the required weight up, and down 2 flights of stairs. The real issue materialised when two females worked together, and had a patient dead or dying, and who they could not treat because they could not get him or her into the ambulance, because they could not lift the patient. They ended up calling for a second vehicle, with 2 people, in order to assist them getting their patient into the ambulance. In my opinion a total waste of time and un- necessary, especially if you employed the right people for

the job in the first instance. In December 2017, my ninety-five-year-old father

had a funny turn. He had chest pain and a chest infection, was pale and sweaty, is arthritic and can barely walk. My mother did not know what to do and, like so many elderly people, who are afraid to call an ambulance, she went outside (she is eighty-six) into the cold, on New Year's Eve, and started to bang on people's doors asking for help.

The third house she knocked on was having a New Year's Eve party, and as luck would have it, most of the people in there were medical students. At least twelve of them escorted my mother back to her house. I don't know why, but most of them had their medical equipment with them. Perhaps they were going to play Doctors and Nurses after the party.

They gave my father the once-over and decided to call an ambulance.

Two young ambulance girls turned up and were given an extensive handover by the medical students.

This is when it went pear-shaped, instead of the ambulance girls using their carry chair to take my father out to the ambulance, they made him walk. Big mistake. Especially when the patient is a known cardiac patient, and the ambulance crew had been given a list of medication by the students, which included cardiac meds.

When a person is interviewed for any Ambulance Service, they are tested on their ability to carry a patient up and down stairs, and when I joined, many of the young girls could not lift and carry a dummy. So what

chance did they have with a real person? When my father was taken home by an ambulance

crew, he was treated in the same manner: he was made to walk, by two ambulance women.

On one occasion, I went to a station on overtime and worked with a female who used to be on my complex. Our very first job was to a gentleman in his eighties. The job was given as a probable CVA (cerebrovascular accident). When we arrived he was upstairs, as soon as I saw the patient, I confirmed he had had a stroke.

My stupid female colleague made him stand up and walk to the staircase. The patient could not move the right side of his body and my colleague tugged at his trousers in order to make him move. Ten minutes passed and we had not reached the top of the staircase.

During those ten minutes, I said that I would go and get the carry chair. Five times I said this, but she was adamant that he could walk. I feared for his life. I had visions of her pulling his trouser leg down each step, and him toppling over and down the stairs. I could bear it no longer, I told him to stay where he was until I came back with a chair.

That put her in a bad mood all night. Needless to say, I never worked with her again, especially as I was on overtime, I could pick and choose who I wanted to work with on overtime, on every other occasion, if you never wanted to work with someone you had to have a valid reason not to.

I knew that any women who worked on the Patient Transport Service (PTS) were capable of lifting and carrying patients, unlike the skinny young girls, who if

they could not make the patient walk, would ask Control to send another crew to assist them. They could have contributed indirectly to a death because of this.

There was a relief, who thought very highly of himself, he was on our complex, which means two or more stations, under the control of one officer. No one thought much of him because of his attitude. One particular summer's day he started work at 7a.m., at Lavender Hill. He only worked half a day, which was odd – maybe he owed them half a day –then spent the next six hours in the pub just down the road from our station.

He got absolutely shit-faced, plastered, and returned to Lavender Hill Station in that state. He said he was going to wait for his girlfriend to turn up, before going out with her.

My crew-mate and I were informed that after having waited for his girlfriend for thirty minutes, he decided to take an ambulance, to go and collect his girlfriend from Wimbledon train station.

He collected her and drove back to Lavender Hill Station, drunk. Even worse is that he took an active ambulance from the station, leaving a crew without an ambulance, who could have been given a job.

He was reckless in other ways in his duties. Once on overtime I worked with him and we went to a diabetic, who was hypoglycaemic. These patients quite often struggle through no fault of their own, so it is quite difficult giving them a jab, or putting something sugary into their mouth. My crew-mate would just inject them through their coat, jumper, t-shirt or vest and think nothing of it. This was very unprofessional, and he could have picked up

germs from his coat and injected him with them. In my opinion it was a very stupid thing to do. Diabetes is usually easily controlled if the sufferer sticks to their regime, of taking their meds, but on the odd occasion, they get caught out.

Our station officer heard about the incident, of taking the ambulance and driving drunk, and instead of making an example of him, they just swept it under the carpet. When you have useless managers, it filters down and reflects on other staff.

Fire

Silent and violent,

Heat ...strokes your body,

Caressing you ... gently,

Warming you ... until bubbles appear,

And burst, and leak,

Leaving you depleted,

Your body, dies of thirst.

10. Fire.

Fires were one of the worst jobs to get, and a horrible way to die. Most of the time the victim died from smoke inhalation, but if they were unlucky they were burned as well.

One time we received a job to an elderly man, who had had a previous stroke. We arrived just after the brick-heads (firemen). The old boy was in a room at the very top of a large Victorian house. A fire had started but been contained within the room. The ceiling was a bit sooty and the net curtains had burned away, but there was no other damage; the fire had stopped as suddenly, as it had started.

The old boy was still sitting in his chair, but the only parts that remained of him were his thighs, his legs and feet. Even his slippers were intact.

The rest of him had gone, disappeared. No bone. Nothing. Just ash.

It was the first time I had ever seen anything like that. Spontaneous combustion; that's what it was. Unbelievable.

JC and I were working a night shift. It was our second night, and we had just dropped a patient off at St Thomas's. It was a dark, damp December night. The little sun we'd had that day had disappeared at 15.30, along with the rain.

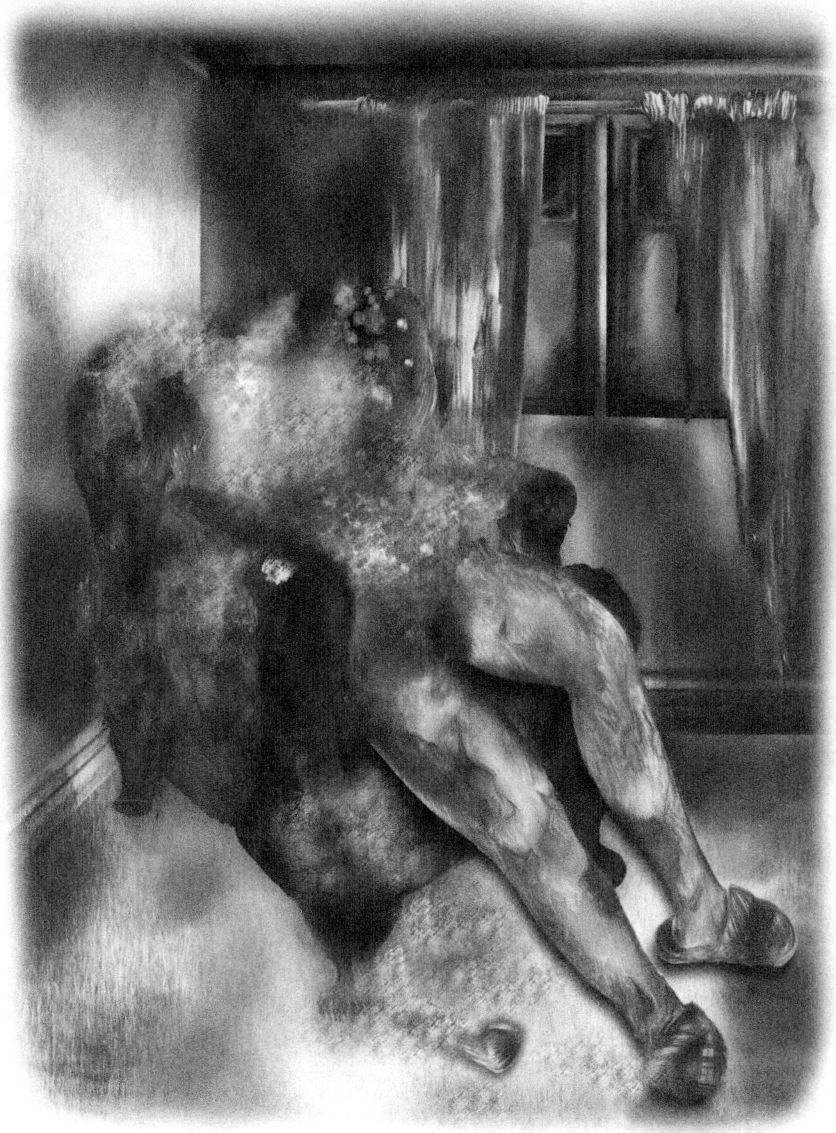

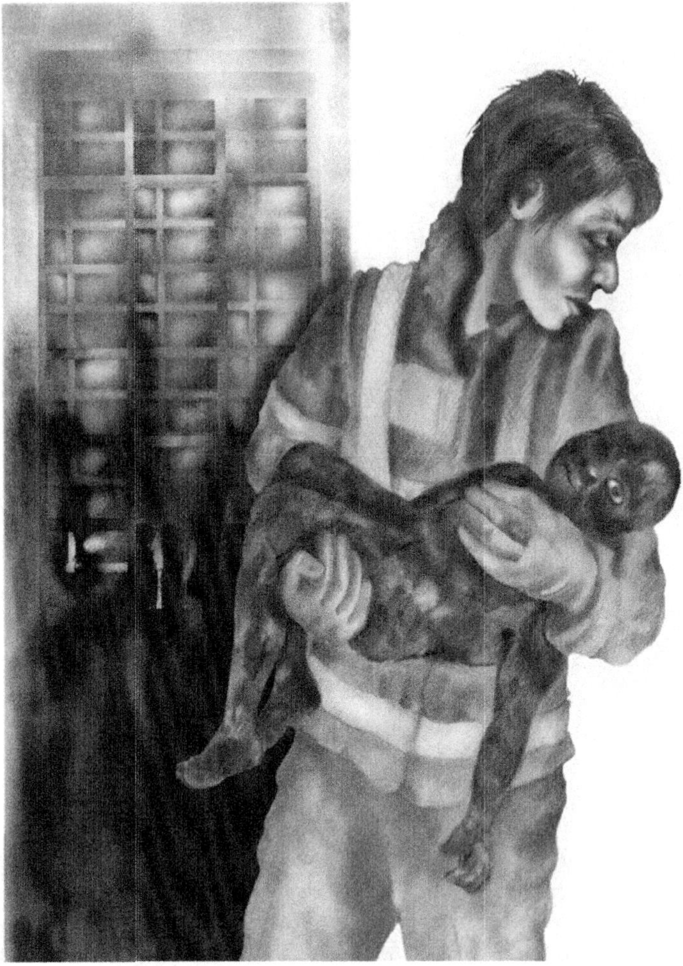

The time was 23.03. We were having a cup of coffee, at St Thomas's, when Control put out a broadcast for a fire. JC was quick on the buzzer: the first to call up, to offer our assistance. He was after a rush again.

If JC could jump onto a proper job, he would, without any hesitation.

The job was to a block of flats, in South-East London: a fire on the fifth floor, with seven persons reported, all with burn injuries.

I drove quickly and we arrived to a scene of total mayhem. Crowds had gathered, people were wailing. The Emergency Services carried on doing their job. Six ambulances were already there and the brick-heads were there in force, as were the police.

The place was like a living nightmare. Smoke filled the air. It was almost overwhelming. The air was acrid. The fire had been put out. The crowds had grown and were everywhere. A TV crew and reporters had arrived.

We saw a Brixton Hill crew carry out a four-year-old boy. He was dead, burned to a crisp. We could see the bones of his fingers.

We made our way upstairs, to the flat. The air was bitter and pungent, still filled with smoke. We could taste it.

There was something else; a familiar smell; a smell that I had tasted before; like sulphur and charcoal, – the smell of burned hair ... and a sickly BBQ smell.

I was not looking forward to this. The images that my mind conjured up should not be shared, not with anyone. We took what we needed and rushed upstairs, to the flat, bumping into another crew on the way down.

I didn't recognise them, but JC did, and gave them a nod. They were carrying a young female, who was still alive.

We got to our patient: a mother, all blistered, with difficulty breathing. She was actually smoking – there was smoke coming off her body and head. I had never

had a patient alive in this condition. We took her to our ambulance and I gave her a bowl,

as she was coughing up sooty phlegm. We did a quick survey of her body, before covering her in burns dressings, I had to get more from the ambulance that had the dead patient.

There is a formula for calculating a patient's survival rate with burns.

% of body burned + patient's age + 17 for an inhalation injury (which our patient had).

If the total was 140 or more then they would definitely die.

We worked out that she had:

% body burned = 102 + her age 43 + 17 = 162. Anything over 33% of burns, that exceeds patients age will determine whether they live or die. Our patient was definitely going to die.

Even if we were wrong by a small percentage our patient was going to die. I put in a blue call to Guys Hospital while JC gave her fluids. I drove with all my lights on, sirens blaring, with a police escort as well, clearing a path for me.

My eyes were trying to put the fire out in my mind. She had six children.

We arrived and rushed her into Resus. She was still smoking. Doctors carried on with the treatment we had started.

Her body was tortured with blisters, still forming and bursting. They were all over her. She wasn't crying, or moaning; she was in complete shock – she never even tried to ask about her children: four were dead at the scene; all had been brought here. The other two were in Resus, like their mother.

A nurse brought over a large roll of cling film. We had to wrap her in it to keep the fluids in and infection out. It also prevented wounds from drying out. We covered the mother in cling film; her body was mummified in transparency.

We assisted as they were short staffed and neither of us felt that we could leave.

I went out to the ambulance to clean up, while JC went to make us a drink. The smell of burning human flesh and hair hung in the ambulance, like a solid entity, an invisible brick wall that I had to keep walking through. I nearly threw up.

I threw out all the bedding, even the clean blankets and bedding. The hospital could wash it all. I cleaned and wiped down everything else, even the windows, then I sprayed some of our NHS Air freshener, but the smell remained in the ambulance, hanging there as a

reminder of the job we had just finished.

The smell was on us, on our clothes, in our hair, stuck in my nose. Until I could have a bath and wash the smell off me, this was how I and JC would smell until the end of our shift.

We had a few worthless jobs before we finished our shift, and to be honest, I was grateful for the crap jobs. Sometimes it was a relief to not get another serious job for the remainder of a shift.

We finished at 06.00, barely speaking. I could still see the mother, the look of bewilderment on her face, as if she were lost in a maze, faced with six routes to escape, but fire all around the maze, and not knowing which route to take, although her life depended on it.

Even as I write this, I can still see her face, smoking, sitting upright on the bed, as we wrapped her in cling film, her eyes open, but not seeing, lost in her own dark thoughts.

We both left our station, not speaking, going our separate ways. I crept into my house, poured half a glass of whisky and drank it in the shower, before crawling onto bed at 06.45.

I dozed off, exhausted and tried to sleep, still thinking about the fire, the only job on our shift that had been genuine, where we might have made a difference.

But in truth we had both known what the outcome was going to be.

I rose just as the kids came home from school at 15.30 and had a bath to try and wake myself up. I could still smell burning flesh. I put on a fresh uniform, before I had some breakfast, then drove slowly to work, in no rush, thinking about my long weekend. I had nothing planned, and planned to do nothing, but I was looking forward to it.

JC and I arrived at Lavender Hill at the same time. We parked and went up to the mess room. The crew we were going to relieve had just got an emergency transfer, and asked us if we would take an early job. We accepted.

The transfer was from Guys to the Chelsea Burns Unit, in Kings Road – our patient from the night before.

My skin crawled. We were not finished with our lady from East London. We conveyed the mother to the Chelsea and West Burns Unit. She was high on medication; her eyes were closed. Her two children that had been alive, had died that morning, but she never knew. She died the following day. A family of seven ... all dead.

JC found out what had happened from friends in the police. It seems her partner had been involved in selling drugs. Something had happened: he had upset some people from a

rival gang. So they petrol-bombed his flat just as the mother had answered the door. She and her six children had been trapped in the flat. Her partner was out.

I was left with the smells from that night for weeks, and nearly twenty years later, I can still see the mother in my mind's eye, smoke coming off her hair and body.

Such a criminal waste of life.

Last Bike Ride

Out in the sunshine,

Riding your bike,

Carefree, and happy,

Riding fast, on the pavement,

Unflinchingly safe, you thought.

I remember your name,

It was such a shame,

Heartbreakingly sad,

You rode your sphere,

With nothing to fear,

And with no headgear.

11. Last Bike Ride.

We were parked up at St George's, waiting to key in, with either a return to station or another job. One job must have pushed all other jobs off the computer system, and we were marked to have it.

I was driving, so my mate took details: RTA. Lorry vs. bike. Ten-year-old male.

Query unconscious. Name of road. Times.

This was serious. When I say I drove fast, I drove really fast. Even Lewis Hamilton couldn't have caught me. 45 seconds gone. I had a choice: to either take a short cut over a pedestrianized area, which had traffic lights, street signs, people and lamp posts. I wasn't even sure if we would fit through the tiny gap in our big yellow truck. But if I went the other way, it would take at least 10 minutes. That could be the difference between life and death.

All this flashed through my mind. Adrenaline must have pumped through my body, and in seconds my mind was made up. I veered to the right and swung a sharp left, as I took the short cut. I looked at my mate: he was peering through his fingers. I said, 'We made it', but there wasn't much in it.

Ninety seconds gone. I was on a road now, foot down, speed up. I saw police up ahead, a lorry half in the road. I pulled up and jumped out with my mate: one movement.

Only two minutes gone, but a lifetime too late.

We ran to the boy. He lay motionless, his 10 years laid out on the concrete. People stared in shock and disbelief. The lorry driver was crying, as he was questioned by the police.

My crew-mate looked at me, tears welling up. We were both choked at this scene. My mate covered him up in our red blanket. Our Control beeped us. I went to answer it.

'Yes?' I said.

'Report, please. HEMS is waiting.' 'You want a report? The boy is dead.'

She replied, 'Report, please.' As if HEMS could do anything. Control asked me a third time, I realised I needed to tell them a bit more. I said "his brains are on the floor, he's dead."

My little boy was the same age. My crew-mate had a girl the same age. Who was going to tell his parents?

The lorry had turned right into an industrial estate and its rear half was still in the road. The boy riding his bike either never saw the lorry, or saw it late, and crashed into the middle wheels of the lorry.

The lorry had crushed the right-hand side of his body; the left side was intact, un touched, as if he were asleep on a school night, after a busy day.

We were both stood down for a couple of hours but that never helped. In those days when I was working and you went on the radio, to talk to control, make a report, or make a request, everyone heard, even those in other sectors of London, there was no privacy. We both decided it was better to keep busy. Neither of us spoke much for the rest of the day. We finished our shift and left for home.

I drove to a park, sat in my car, and cried for an hour, thinking about the boy and his parents. The incident would affect a great many people, in many ways.

I made my way home, saw my kids, gave them kisses and hugs and put them to bed. Then I told my wife about the job. I couldn't eat, so I had a double whisky, then another, and another, and another. And then I went to bed.

The story made the news on TV, and the press. I read all about the boy and his family. He was an only child, this was tragic, absolutely tragic.

131

One-K

He had headaches,

He looked pale, and sweaty,

He had unknown pains,

That hurt,

He felt ill, and sick with worry,

His wife never knew,

His kids never knew,

His family never knew,

But he knew,

loved by wife, and children,

he could not cope,

He had no hope,

So, he chose to hang,

From a tree in Wandsworth,

My very first hanging, Too scared to touch him, I had to feel, for a pulse, I touched him, cold and hard, Like wax, melted, cooled and hardened, after

flickering its last, tiny flame, He died, for a ... CCJ 1k owed.

(A C.C.J. stands for a county court judgement, this person killed himself for owing £1000.00

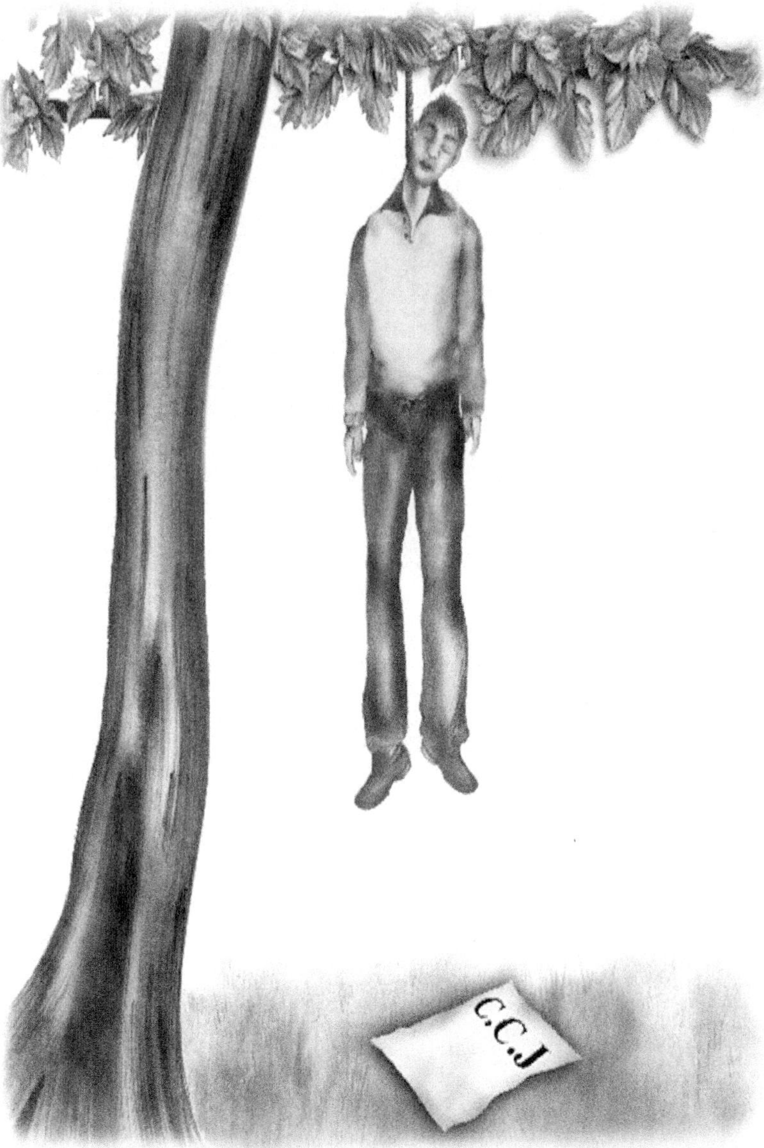
C.C.J

12. Hangings, Suicides and Self-Harm

Suicide was, and possibly still is, the leading cause of death in the UK. The reasons for suicide are too many to go into and I am no expert. But we all have different limits to stress factors, which is why some people will attempt it and some won't.

We often had to attend hangings. We were near to Springfield Psychiatric Hospital and Wandsworth Prison, so all our crews experienced their fair share of hangings.

The problem with attending hangings at Wandsworth Prison was that it could take up to twenty minutes to gain entry. Their security was so high, that by the time six or seven gates had been unlocked then locked, before you could proceed to the next one, the patient did not have a hope in hell of surviving.

If the prisoner had hanged himself, in the vain hope of being found quickly, he would be wrong. That was never going to happen, so most would die. I don't know if their procedure has changed in any way since I was last

there. We encountered all sorts of hangings; some were

really inventive. The problem was that if they didn't do it properly, then the person would suffer an awful death.

Sometimes there was also the odd accident, where some people had practised auto-erotic asphyxiation to heighten their pleasure.

I remember one in Streatham, a woman lying naked on the bed. The man with her just looked at her and hadn't even attempted CPR.

We started resus immediately, as the man, a foreigner, could not – or would not – speak to us in English. We blue-lighted her into St George's. It was only after my handover that I noticed ligature marks around her ankles. I checked her wrists; she had them there as well. It soon became apparent what had been going on: their sexual foreplay had gone a little bit too far.

There were also young girls, who believed they had found the love of their life. When the relationship came to an end for whatever reason, these young teens would become distraught. They couldn't think properly and there was no consoling them. Suddenly they couldn't cope with life and didn't know who to turn to, or what to do.

It could be either of them that could not cope in a relationship – the boy or girl – and they thought that if they hurt themselves, their partner would come back.

But they never did ... and nor did they. They were found by their parents in the morning, hanging in the garden from a clothes line, or some other place in the house: planned with precision and yet the parents hadn't noticed or suspected anything.

It happened to young men as well, or anyone being bullied at school, who was afraid to tell their teacher or their parents. Instead, they decided to find their own way out. People harmed themselves for all sorts of reasons, and it wasn't just limited to the young.

Some youngsters did it because they didn't attain the grades they needed for university. One of the biggest reasons for hanging among males was debt. We are all different. Some people are unable to cope with the idea of being in debt, and some people couldn't care less.

Today I believe many people live with considerable

debt. A woman from Streatham hanged herself from the balustrade at the top of her of staircase, after finding out her husband had been cheating on her. We all react differently: others could walk away from any situation and never look back and it would never affect them.

A boy of fifteen tied a noose around his neck and tied the other end to the balcony railings of a second floor flat. He was home alone, made no phone calls and left no note. Nothing. He then jumped to his death. No one ever found out why.

I remember picking up a man who had lost his job and was going to be evicted from his tied accommodation. He fell into a deep depression, felt he had nothing left to live for and had contemplated suicide, by burning down the house in which he was living. He phoned a good friend of his to offer him some furniture, right before carrying out his intentions.

His friend knew something was wrong, so they talked and he persuaded him not to follow through, with his actions and to seek help. I ended up going to this chap on several occasions. He never sought help immediately. Instead, he started to cut himself with razor blades or a Stanley knife. He showed us the cuts, as we could see the blood stains on his jeans.

He said he had nearly 300 cuts on his thighs; that it was like a release from his problems and helped to make him feel alive. He believed it made him feel better. So, he cut whenever he felt low. The problem is that this type of release can become addictive for many people.

The tops of his legs were hidden from the world. If you'd seen him, you would not have thought that he was doing such a thing. But how well do we really know people? Even those closest to us?

This chap got the help he needed, and we never saw him again. I hope that's a good sign.

But can you imagine how many people out there finish work, or school, and go home,

pretending to be happy, putting on their masks when they go out for all to see, and yet when they return home and go to bed, or sit in front of the TV, they begin to cry or cut.

full of · Legs: · broken · cut · I lie. · pain · I'm smiling · fears · lonely nights · demons · don't feel alive · Arms · my self · heavy · Brain · scars. · Lungs: · suicidal · I smiled · hard to breathe. · depressed · cuts. · emotions · Heart · I'm breathing · deepest · fought · just scars · Mouth: · insecurities · Eyes · too many tears · I · insults · but · can't contain · stupid · beating

In reality, it could all be because of our way of life, how we live, what's expected of us, problems with love, money, break-ups, children.

There is far less communication between people these days. Everyone is in a rush, only concerned with looking after their own selfish interests.

Maybe that's just how it is now.

My very first hanging was to a man who owed £1,000. After searching for a pulse, I found in his pocket, a County Court Judgement for £1,000.

At least three times per week, we would be called to attempted suicides. This illustrates the magnitude of the problem: if you imagine 350 ambulances and consider that one-third of them are going to psychiatric calls every day, with some of those people actually killing or harming themselves, then if you transfer that to the whole country ... the numbers are staggering.

Some of them chose to hang off balconies, twenty floors up, threatening to jump.

Some actually did. We didn't have the training to try and talk them down, but if we were on scene first, then we would.

We would also have to undertake psychiatric Sections, to assist the police. These were quite sad, as some people seemed fine on our first meeting. I could not, and would not, argue with a doctor or social worker, so I looked on, keeping my thoughts to myself.

We all must have looked overwhelmingly intimidating to one young patient. She was fourteen and was going to be sectioned to Springfield Hospital. I remember her begging her mother, saying, 'Mum, why are you doing this? I'm okay. There's nothing wrong with me.'

I stood there quietly, just looking at the daughter, then the mother. Both were visibly upset. The girl had been violent to herself and others, and had once thrown a TV out of the window at passers-by. That was probably reason enough to warrant a section.

She carried on pleading; her mother carried on crying. The psychiatrist broke the stalemate by saying we need to go. People never went willingly; it usually ended up with the police forcing the patient into the ambulance. These jobs were very costly and tied up a lot of professional staff for some time. This particular job ended up with the girl being handcuffed and removed.

At other times we would have to go to a place of work to remove an unsuspecting patient. I remember one, at an industrial estate. He never saw us all arrive in force. He was working and looked fine, but he probably had problems outside of work. When he spotted us, he made a run for it. We watched as eight huge coppers,

with no tact in their back pockets, just brute strength, grabbed him unceremoniously. His work colleagues looked on perplexed.

I wasn't impressed how this was going. It was a huge struggle, as they all jumped on him. I screamed at them to get off his chest. It wouldn't have been the first time police had, in a similar situation, smothered the patient with their body weight and suffocated a patient, killing him. I was not going to allow that. This is the main reason that we had to accompany police on sections, for patient protection. We also had to accompany police, for their protection, when they went out on raids.

Sometimes we were called to an overdose. My crew-mate and I knew what to do. We would revert to our good cop–bad cop routine. Invariably we ended up making our patient laugh. It was often women who chose pills as their method of choice to die; men chose hanging. An overdose was a painless method, unless they opted for aspirin, which was a very painful way to die. By the time we arrived, most of the overdose patients were already suffering the consequences, as the tablets had been absorbed into their bloodstream.

Our job was to try and give them the best possible outcome, with the necessary care they needed. Most who try to commit suicide don't want to die, they just don't want to live either. I never really understood that.

Maybe they could find no way out of their current situation, hence the contradictory statements. It was a cry for help. The good cop–bad cop routine worked with most patients and we would take them to hospital. Some we couldn't and usually we had to leave them, as

kidnapping wasn't in our remit. Some patients would speak, others stayed silent and just stared at the floor.

Terminal illness is, in my opinion, a valid reason for assisted suicide. After all, we do it for our pets, so why not for our loved ones?

Drugs are another reason, some kill themselves. A friend I had many years ago, took some LSD. She had taken it several times, without any problem, but on one occasion, while waiting for an Underground train to arrive, she jumped up intending to launch herself in front of the train. She later told me that she had no reason to jump; the thought just entered her head to jump. She said that if her friend had not touched her arm, she would have jumped and probably died.

There have also been cases of people thinking they could fly when under the influence of LSD. Many people in the 1970s found out they couldn't.

144

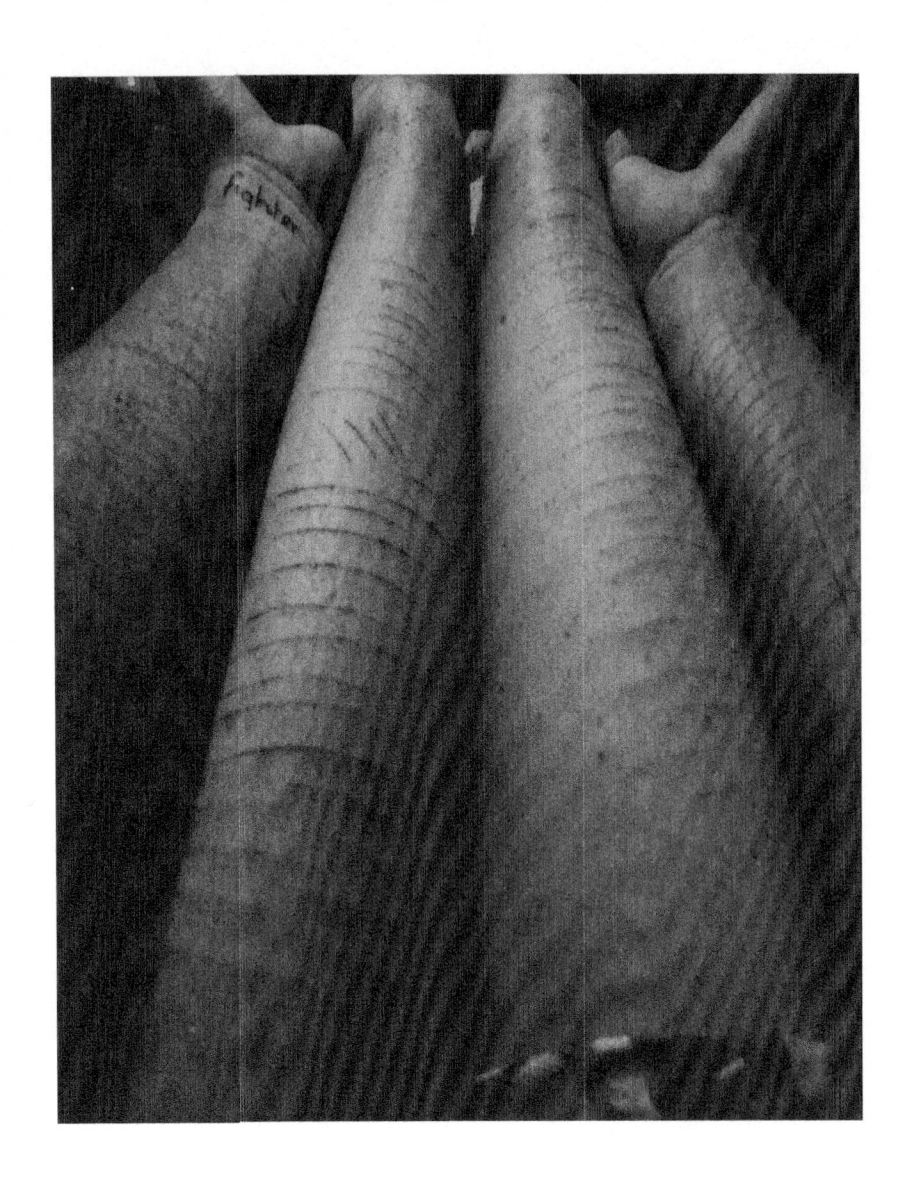

Sometime Soon

Sometime soon,

I may feel different ... better

Better ... about myself?

Better ... about my life?

Better about people,

Better ... about my situation?

Better ... about the future,

but It's a problem,

A problem that needs to be resolved,

Sometime soon.

there will be a new moon,

Sometime soon, I need help,

But it's odd, that God,

Cannot hear my cries,

Only my sighs,

And the shaky sound of my tears,

he hears.

 Life goes on,

I follow the footsteps of my shadow,

Not knowing where it leads,

I just follow the hollow sounds of my steps,

They take me to an old familiar place,

Where I look for the gentle release,

Of my torment,

My anx in my pants, (haha)

I look for the sharpness of the razor,

or my old friend Stanley,

I tried the scissors,

How stupid can I be? They hurt!

A man of my age acting like a young girl,

Who is in a tizz,

About a useless boyfriend, who she believes she loves,

a man of my age,

who knows better,

who should be able to deal with problems,

In a rational way, and yet, ... can't,

because he's tried.

I have tried and nothing helps

except the cuts.

Cutting across the grain,

Releasing the little fountain of red,

Slowly ooooooozing out of my legs,

Hidden from prying eyes,

they ... That think they know me.

How little they know me,

Or my life,

How little anyone cares for the ill,

who're given lots of pills,

to stop the thoughts, And the shakes,

Let Stanley, Slowly stroke my leg,

Enticing my pain to be released,

Easing my pain ... not too deep,

But deep enough to hurt,

Deep enough To hear my silent scream,

To scar,

But never deep enough to die,

Or go to hospital.

I take care of myself,

a fortune spent on aid,

A number spent on cleaning.

  I counted them one day,

The scars,

The latitudes, And the longitudes,

I counted them.

250 at the last,

A year ago,

Sometimes, I cut in the old scar,

So that I don't get a new scar,

A man of my age, how stupid am I?

And yet comfort resides In the smile, of the cuts,

if only for a day.

Sometime soon,

maybe …

Maybe ….

sometime … soon …

Help Me, Please

I called for your help,

late one night,

I was in pain,

you came ...

read my notes,

You ignored my pleas for help,

I struggled,

My legs twitched,

I couldn't fight back

you ended my life

with a pillow.

13. God in the Ambulance Service

How do you begin a story like this? I swear to tell the whole truth, and nothing but the truth? That's good enough.

Around the end of July, I was off work. I had been involved in a crash and had a shoulder injury, so was attending St Thomas's hospital, for physio and to have an injection to help with the pain. It's a great hospital, especially for its location, right opposite the Houses OF Parliament. It has great views, especially from the 20th floor.

There are always lots of people milling around, and has a vibrancy not normally associated with a hospital; like a happy event, a festival. People had medical appointments there, but they made a day of it. I thought it a bit weird – I could think of better things to do than to hang around a hospital.

I finished my appointment and decided to pop into my station, to see who was around, have a chat and a coffee with them. I drove to Lavender Hill station. There was one ambulance parked up, so one crew on

station. I went in and saw Harry puffing furiously on a cigarette. Immediately, I knew something was up. We all got upset by some jobs; it just depended on what it was, and what our triggers were for them to affect us.

Harry was smoking a fresh fag as I made my way up the stairs towards him. He looked like a frightened child, and was repeating the same words, looking left and right, not looking at me. I did not need to be a detective to know something was wrong.

I asked, 'What's wrong, mate?'

He turned and faced me. He was in bits, crying, sucking on his cigarette. He was saying, 'She killed him. She fucking killed him'

I said, 'Who? What? Did you have a suspended patient (a cardiac arrest)?' 'No,' he said.

I said. 'For fucks sake, just tell me.' 'She suffocated him,' he answered.

I asked who he was working with, although I had already guessed. I was right, he was working with Jan. A bitch. No one liked her. Why he'd ever crewed up with that bitch, I will never know.

I asked him what had happened. Harry was a big bloke; he never spoke much.

He started to open up, as he lit another fag, and said they'd got a call to an elderly man. I was hoping he'd speak quicker before Jan came out, and he clammed up for good.

He said he was driving, when they got to the job, so she went in first, while he got a chair and blanket, in preparation to take the patient to hospital. He said when he got to the

bedroom, she was sitting astride him, suffocating him with a pillow. He said he just stood there, mouth open, wordless. He said nothing and did nothing, he felt nailed to the floor.

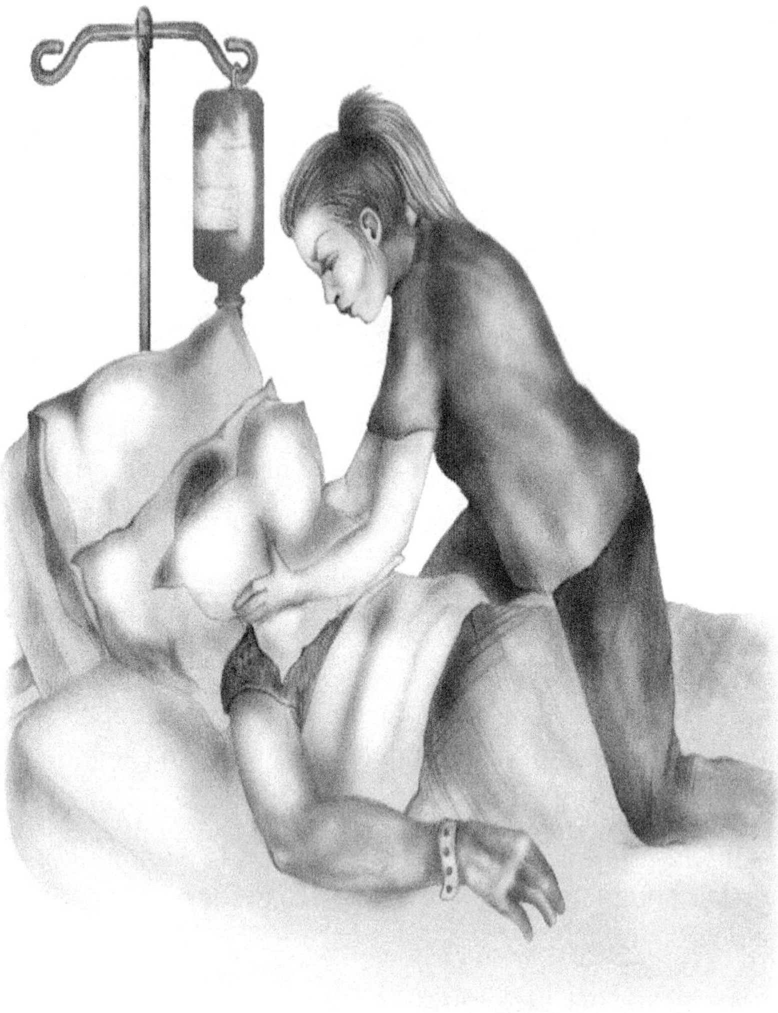

The consequences ... Lie No. 1: Jan had to inform our Control that the patient was suspended [see above] before they got there, and so they never attempted resus.

Lie No. 2: They had to call for a GP to come and certify death. Then they had to wait for a police officer to relieve them before leaving the job. While they waited for the doctor to arrive, she completed her paperwork.

Lie No. 3: The doctor came and asked her what happened. She informed him the patient was dead before they arrived. Lie No. 4: The police officer arrived after the doctor

had left. He asked questions as well, and as cool as a cucumber she told the same story.

He lit another fag and told me when she went to see the patient, his medical notes were on the side, she scanned them quickly and saw he had a few serious problems, and in her wisdom, and god-like standing, she decided that he would be better off dead.

He lit another fag, and blew poison in my face, then repeated that as he had entered the bedroom, she was sitting on top of the patient, pushing a pillow into his face. The man was still struggling – a natural response to suffocation.

I was shocked, but not that shocked.

Surely a patient calling an ambulance meant he wanted help? He had not called them to put him to sleep ... forever.

I told him that he needed to report this immediately, otherwise he could become an accessory to premeditated murder.

The bitch came out, gave me a filthy look, and stared at Harry for a long time, telling him with her eyes not to say anything. Then she went back to the mess room. She had to have been listening.

I told him he couldn't work with her. She was dangerous, and he needed to report it straightaway today.

He just looked at me and lit another fag.

Finally, I said, 'Listen, Harry, you've just involved me in all this. So either you report her by tomorrow or I'll report both of you. You shouldn't have told me, because now I have to do something about it.'

He lit another fag as I made my way out, to my car, and I called out to him that I would ring him in the morning.

I rang him in the morning, but he never took my advice, so I went to see my station officer and reported what had happened. He was not impressed with me for telling him. He was casual about it. It was an evil act, but he took no notice.

For a caring profession, I was amazed at how uncaring the senior management was.

I was not surprised by what Harry had told me. I had heard rumours about staff doing stuff like this: murder on the cheap. I wondered if she had done this before with her previous partners, after all you don't just suddenly turn up at a job and decide to murder someone, do you? People she was crewed up with did not stay with her for long, and left. I began to wonder what had caused her other partners to stop working with her.

After all, there are instances of nurses and doctors, who had killed patients as well, so why would I be surprised if one or some of our staff killed patients.

So, I wasn't surprised, but I was shocked, maybe because it was on my doorstep; maybe because I was a third party to the fact. I wondered just how big a problem it was in the

whole of the NHS, or how widespread it was in the caring professions. Was it just London staff who had succumbed to this level? I went to the police, I gave them date, time, and

names and a full account of what had been said. I could do no more.

They were questioned and they said they had played a practical joke on me. Control informed the police that they had never been called out to an elderly man and the police took their word.

What had I expected? What service would admit to their staff playing God and killing a patient. A patient who had called for their help. I just felt that this was another cover up.

From that day on, I informed all my family and friends that they should never let their elderly relatives be alone when an ambulance was called.

Who could you trust, if you couldn't trust those sent to help?

14. Pranks, Drink, Drugs and Sex

Everyone at Lavender Hill enjoyed playing pranks, even the women, although they never, ever came out on top. They would try and spike your drinks with all kinds of things ranging from various forms of chilli, both fresh and bottled, through to laxatives, including chocolate laxatives. They would take these out of the wrapper and put them on a plate with other sweets and chocolates.

Diarrhoea was something we all had at some point. Some clever dick, found a clear, colourless and tasteless liquid that they could add to people's drinks, to make them have a real shitty day. This made everyone refuse drinks from anyone who offered to make them. In the end we all made our own, until one day we'd forget and accept a drink from someone else. Then we suffered.

It was 1st April; a dangerous day for any emergency worker. We could not trust anyone, not even our own crew-mate. JC and I were in at 06.00, ready for a 12-hour shift. We checked our vehicle all over, including under our seats and the bonnet where we, or others, might place fresh fish in the girls' ambulances.

Satisfied that we were safe, we made our own drinks and chilled out, as we waited for the phone to ring. We had just finished our tea when it rang. We started the day with an eighty-eight-year-old cardiac arrest. He had been found by the warden at the sheltered housing, fifteen minutes after the patient sounded his alarm.

This was a definite no deal, this one is dead and is staying dead. We did what we could for him, I went through the motions while JC blued us to St George's. He was intubated and we had given him drugs, but there was nothing on the defibrillator, just a nice, long, black, flat line.

We took him to Resus. They too went through the motions, as it was the only way junior doctors and nurses could get real experience on a real body; it was good practice. It's just a fact. They went through the motions for twenty minutes, then called it.

Unlike Mayday Hospital in Croydon. If you arrived with a cardiac arrest, they would ask the patient's age first, anyone over sixty, they would tell you to take them straight to the mortuary. I found that disgusting. There was no chance for an elderly person, and how could junior staff ever learn, and get real practice?

I hope they have changed this practice now.

I went and booked the old boy in and suggested we go and get some breakfast. JC agreed. He liked the idea, as he was always hungry. We went out to the vehicle and saw the

old boy's shoes and hat. I had an idea. I suggested we make up the bed, fill the middle with rolled-up blankets, put the shoes at the end of the stretcher and place the hat at the top end. Then we should go and get some breakfast, as we

pushed the stretcher through the hospital, just to see what happened and watch people's reactions.

So that's what we did. I was cracking jokes. JC was laughing out loud and people were giving us filthy looks. The hospital was busy with people starting work. One lady came up to us and shouted, 'You should be disgusted with yourselves. You have no respect for the dear departed! Don't you care?'

When she'd finished her tirade, we both burst out laughing and then a few seconds later, I threw off the cover. She laughed too and laughed all the way down the corridor. Others joined in once they realised it was 1st April and just a practical joke.

We got back to station. There were eight of us, as well as the station officer. He had come down to give us our personal issue radios – something we needed. The station officer said there was fresh tea in the pot. We didn't suspect anything. We both got our mugs and poured our tea. JC sat down. I looked around. I was being looked at ... or I thought I was.

JC and I both drank our tea, putting it to our mouth at the same time. 'Fuck!' I shouted.

JC shouted, 'Bollocks!'

The mess room was awash with laughter. They had bought the hottest chillies they could find and rubbed them around the rim of our mugs. I had never seen our station officer laugh: that was a sight to behold.

We joined in with the laughter, but I was already thinking about how I could get them back for this.

We too were given our radios. Everyone had them switched on. I went to the changing room and filled up a bucket with water. Then I went to the toilet, switched my radio on and just dribbled some water into the toilet bowl. Then I poured more in, then slowed it down.

I did this for a good five minutes then went back to the mess room, where they were all laughing at me. They'd heard everything and shouted, 'What's wrong with your bladder?'

I just joined in with them. It was always a good crack on station. There was a great camaraderie, at our station, more than at other stations.

Only the Emergency services and the armed forces had this kind of camaraderie, not other professions. We all knew how to treat each other. When a crew had a really nasty job, we knew that the others would understand. We were definitely a close-knit unit at Lavender Hill, and I feel privileged to have worked, with most of the people on that station.

Everyone slipped back into relaxation mode, as the station officer left.

Not even five minutes had passed before the phone rang: four crews, four jobs: an urgent, two assists, and JC and I got the drunks in Battersea.

We knew these two – both alcoholics, we had nicknamed Little and Large. Large was nearly 7foot tall, with his large black boots; the other was 4ft 11in. The tall one, Roger, kept hitting the smaller one, Tim. He would take all his benefit money and bully him. They shared a flat and were outside there. I went inside with Tim, while JC stayed outside with Roger. I cleaned up his minor injury, then proceeded to give him some self- defence lessons.

Roger was drunk on Tim's money, whereas Tim was still sober, so he listened intently. I told him, if Roger started on him, he had to punch him in the nuts, with all his strength. Then when his head came down, he had to punch him on the chin, using all his strength. He would then fall on the floor where he could give him a couple of kicks.

Hopefully Roger wouldn't ever bother him again.

It wasn't in our remit to teach self-defence, but if it reduced our calls from these two, then it wasn't a bad thing. [You might find that this is a little controversial given the position you were in at the time.

Late one night, in January, when it had been snowing, JC was outside having a smoke when he saw two female police officers, who used to come in for a coffee. They were on a job right opposite our station. JC phoned me and told me to get all the crews down, so we could snowball the cops.

There were six of us on station, and it 02.00 on a Tuesday night, so it was getting quiet. We just had to do this; it was too good an opportunity to miss. We all crept behind the ambulances and made several snowballs each.

JC gave a nod, and we pelted the cops with iced snowballs. They shouted for us to stop, and kept saying, 'We're on a job', but we didn't listen. We just battered them with more snowballs, and continued to do so until they left.

We went back to the mess room, laughing out loud.

The policewomen wouldn't be coming back anytime soon. After doing a few more jobs we sat back in the mess room, ready for a bit of shut-eye, when the doorbell rang. It was 04.00. JC was smoking in the corridor, so he went to see who it was. The policewomen had come back to give us a bit of payback.

Before JC knew what was happening, he had been handcuffed and frogmarched upstairs. JC was laughing hysterically. They cuffed him to the staircase and said to the rest of us: 'Come down and take some photos of him.' So we did, and that was our big mistake.

One of them was upstairs with the fire hose and the other was armed with another downstairs. They turned the hoses on and the pressure of the water pushed us to the floor.

We ended up so wet, it was like we'd had a bath with our clothes on. 'Who's laughing now?' they said.

Most of us didn't have clean clothes on station, so we remained wet till our shift ended.

Before the policewomen left, I offered them coffee, which they accepted. JC spiked it

with laxatives, so we had the last laugh.

Before I left, in the morning, I put Amphiset (an alcohol disinfectant) in Billy's aftershave. He always came in early and had the same daily routine: shit, shower and a shave.

I sat in my car waiting for an indication he'd used his aftershave. I quickly drove off when I heard the earth shattering scream.

Steve was the king of practical jokes. He once made a life-size cut-out of a man out of cardboard, climbed onto the roof of the ladies changing room, and placed it, face- down on the opaque glass roof. When the ladies gazed up, they saw a person looking down at them. It was very realistic. One time the police were called only to discover it was a cardboard cut-out.

Another one he was renowned for, was sticking cling film across the toilet bowl, causing a big splash back. He did it to the gents' loo as well, which caused a few problems.

Whenever women were on station, we made sure we had fresh fish, and hid it all over their ambulances so they wouldn't find it all and would have to suffer the smell all shift. That always gave us a good laugh.

We were also armed with spud guns in the winter, and water bombs and water pistols in the summer. We used to have the odd great battle with each other.

Writing this down on paper makes us sound childish, and maybe we were, but the reason for this pranks was that, they were a release from the traumatic jobs we often had to attend.

Otherwise we would have gone mad. So they lightened the mood in between our serious episodes.

Our fun and silly side never ever affected the quality of our patient care. Our patients' care always came first.

We had days when most of our jobs were a total waste of time. During these periods, the crews would give different initials. When we received a crap job, Control would have to repeat our initials. We had great fun making them up, and some used their real ones, adding their middle initial which made a word. It may sound silly, but it gave us all a laugh on these boring days. These are some of them.

Gulf–Oscar–Delta = god

Sierra–India–Romeo = sir.

Foxtrot– Charlie–Kilo = f_ck

Kilo–Alpha–Kilo = kak.

Kilo–Oscar–Kilo = kok

Delta–India–Kilo =dik

Tango–India–Tango = tit

Papa–Oscar–Oscar = poo.

Sierra–Hotel–Tango = s_ht

Alpha–Romeo–Sierra–Echo = arse.

The list went on and on, and just got more creative.

Every Christmas there were parties, we could go to, if we weren't working. Everyone let loose at Christmas, with most gagging for easy, uncomplicated sex. Not only did we have to deal with the drunks throughout the year, but come Christmas we also had our fair share of NHS drunks.

I remember one year, at Lavender Hills Christmas do I watched Stavros smuggle in a bottle of whisky; cheap rubbish only good for getting merry. None of us earned much money, so I can see why he brought his own. I watched him eating squid and drinking whisky. He was really enjoying himself. An hour later, his station officer called our main station and got an ambulance to take him home.

He was taken outside to wait for the ambulance and within a minute he projectile- vomited squid rings, and tentacles, swimming in a sea of green whisky and ginger.

I swear I could see the tentacles moving. When they got him to his house, they pushed him in

and shut the door. Next morning his wife found him asleep on the hallway floor. She woke him up and asked him why he hadn't come to bed and he replied that he couldn't find the stairs.

He never got drunk again.

I never realised, but at our main station there were a lot of coke heads and addicts. Some would use drugs meant for patients. St George's hospital always had a great party. One year I downed a couple of bourbons and then settled down with a ginger ale, so that it looked like I was drinking something alcoholic. I watched as about six blokes flew into the men's loo.

I thought there might be a fight or something, so I went to have a look, and there they all were, snorting lines of coke, with £10 notes. It was a drug den. They were all sniffing white powder up their nostrils,

I was offered some, but declined saying I was happy with bourbon. I left. I never needed drugs to enjoy myself, I functioned fine with alcohol in moderate doses.

Two days later I went to the main station for some overtime. There was a guy who never usually drove, which I thought was odd I used to prefer a day of each, as driving released me from the monotony of having to listen to someone moan about a tiny ailment.

Driving also offered the opportunity to drift into my own thoughts, albeit just for the 10–15 minutes it took to get to hospital. It was a release, so I wondered why he never drove. I soon found out.

We were sent on standby to St George's. It was a Saturday morning, about eight o'clock. He didn't speak much and then he spied a pigeon in distress. He asked me to stop and rescued the pigeon, then asked me to go to the Blue Cross (an animal charity), as it was on the way. I did, but it seemed a bit OTT.

That's when I started to scrutinise his every action. We got to the Blue Cross and he rang the doorbell persistently. I'm pretty sure he pissed them off, especially as they were closed on a Saturday. He had a glazed look in his eyes, and I thought to myself, He's a user. He's on something. That's why he doesn't want to drive.

We left there after they'd thanked him sarcastically and copped a job before reaching St George's, for a forty-year-old, suspended, in Balham. The patient was on the top floor of a building that was being refurbished. We arrived and were met by a policewoman. She was very casual and I judged by her inaction that the patient was past our assistance.

As soon as she told us he was a night security guard, I formed an opinion as to what may have happened. She took us upstairs. I had the defibrillator ready, my crew- mate had his tool-bag. I touched the patient: he was as hard as rock; his pupils were fixed and dilated.

I asked the cop if the petrol heater was on. I'd already guessed that it was, as it was quite warm for a building that had no windows. The pigeon fancier told me to start resus.

I looked at the cop, who gave me a quizzical look, as if to say, 'What for?'

I said to him, 'What the fuck for? Are you stupid? He's been dead for hours.' I suspected that he had lain down for a bit of shut-eye, fallen asleep with the heater on and asphyxiated as a result of carbon monoxide poisoning. It was a painless way to go: doze off; no pain; no worry; just nothingness.

I argued with the pigeon fancier, but four times he reiterated that I should start CPR. I walked away with the policewoman, who was also eager to leave. Before we left, I connected the patient to the defibrillator and printed off a strip that showed him to be flat-lined, then I threw it at my crew-mate and walked away. I never worked with him again.

I found out a couple of years later that he and several others had been kicked out for drug abuse.

Sex ... what a great word, sex is. It conjures up nice feelings and sex was still free – the Government had not yet found a way to tax, sex. Shift work was the cause of many a relationship break-up. It was just a fact of life: two ships passing each other, day and night, beginning to drift apart. Sexual appetite, loneliness, closeness, opportunity and the need to have sex when you wanted, all added to couples' breaking up.

The Emergency services just added another dimension to these feelings, by placing their workers in a big club, where new friendships were formed, with and without sex. This added to the pressures of stable couples breaking up, especially when one, or both, had a career change and moved into one of the Emergency services.

People need to understand that emergency workers are a special group of people. It's not for everyone, but for those who make it their chosen profession, it makes them special, just by their devotion and the nature of their work.

I remember one night we were parked up at St Thomas's, when I saw Jeff from our complex, I asked him who he was working with and he said he was with Mark. When I asked where Mark was, he replied that he was in the ambulance having sex with one of the nurses. We crept over to his ambulance, and sure enough, we could see them, stark naked, going at it like rabbits.

Another night we were at Chelsea and West, after taking a patient there. We grabbed a coffee and stood outside as it was a warm night. I looked round and there were seven other ambulances parked up. I said to JC, 'Those two over there in the corner are shaking. You don't think someone's taking a private blood pressure, do you?'

He said, 'Come on, let's take a look.'

Sure, enough there were another four rabbits in the two ambulances. I said to JC that desperation must have set in. I went to the canteen and asked the cooks for two whole carrots, which I placed under their windscreen wipers.

It was no different on some stations, especially our main one, Wimbledon Hill, where people were shagging sometimes on night shifts. I wondered if I had lost my libido, or did I just like my creature comforts, preferring a bed to an ambulance?

168

15. Surfing in Morden

Rain fell steadily, like a tap turned on; a constant steady dripping, like Chinese water torture. It rained for three days and three nights. I was on overtime at Wimbledon Hill with Jeff, and we were working lates: 15.00–23.00. Jeff and I were second out, as we had just returned from St George's.

We managed to cop our first job for one of our regulars, whose name was Jock – that's all we knew about him. He was an alcoholic, NFA (no fixed abode). He had previously been a 'walker', but had now advanced into a wheelchair through illness, drinking and drugs. In addition, now he was a diabetic, had heart problems and was a double amputee, with a colostomy bag.

We took him to St George's, and got a return immediately. It seemed to be a quiet night for everyone. I think the nursing staff were pleased too. We sat on station for an hour. Jeff was fidgeting, I could tell he was bored; he just wanted a job. The quietness never bothered me, I just looked at it, as easy overtime. Jeff and I were used to being run off our feet, but the difference was that I could enjoy a quiet night and he couldn't.

We sat there, eyes half-closed, watching crap on TV. In the end we both closed our eyes and went into Lavender Hill relaxation mode, conserving our energy for whatever the night might throw at us.

The other crew were a right pair; one was a Viking – Nigel, what sort of name was that for a Viking? His partner was Bruce, the Lech. Jeff had worked overtime with the Viking at Wimbledon Hill. One night, they had a call to a young lady, in her twenties. The call was local, not far from the station. She had apparently sleepwalked straight off her balcony and fallen 20ft while asleep, before she hit the ground. Her balcony was at the front of the house, with metal railings on the boundary. She fell between the railings and the house, into the basement area. She could have died, or impaled herself, on the railings.

Jeff was attending to the patient and put a cervical collar on the patient, while he waited for the Viking to bring more equipment. The Viking came back with a chair and a blanket. What the hell was Viking thinking? The patient possibly had neck, head, and back injuries and possible fractures, so bringing a chair and a blanket was like going to someone with an arterial bleed, and giving them a plaster to stick on a wound, that was spurting blood.

Jeff put the Viking right and told him to get another crew for assistance. The Viking wasn't liked by anyone, wherever he worked. When he had left his previous station, Highgate Hill, he had held some kind of pagan ritual, placing candles on the ground and then reciting

some kind of gibberish, putting a curse on everyone

who worked there. That's when he put in for a transfer to Wimbledon Hill.

The other bloke, Bruce the Lech, wasn't liked either. No one worked with either of them willingly. It seemed fitting that they were paired together for the night. Bruce was always perving at patients, nurses, and colleagues. He went to a PV (vaginal) bleed once (I remember it well, there were two crews there, but I can't remember why) and insisted that the patient went into the bathroom to remove the pad, so that he could examine it. What medical reason could anyone possibly have, to want to look at a bloody pad? He was a joke. He left after a couple of years and joined the police force.

The phone rang. Jeff's eyes opened as the Norseman took the call: thirty-year-old male. Cardiac arrest. No history of previous illness. No resus in progress.

Jeff told Nigel to ask Control if we could go as a second crew. It made sense, as two people dealing with a cardiac arrest is difficult and not as effective, especially with those two. We were given permission. The job was local and we could be there in 3/4 minutes. We arrived together and rushed into the house with our equipment. There were more than twenty people in the house, as there was some kind of celebration going on. They were just standing there, looking at their friend, or relative, dead on the floor.

We were told that he had flown in from Australia that morning. It sounded like a possible DVT (deep vein thrombosis). I wired the patient to our defibrillator, while Jeff intubated. Bruce did chest compressions. Viking got the stretcher ready and we were nearly ready

to leave. Jeff gave the patient some adrenaline, and we managed to get a shockable rhythm, but after shocking him, there was no change, so we decided to go to St Georges.

We loaded the patient in the Lech's truck. Jeff would go with them and I would convey some relatives. I took five relatives with me and made my way steadily to St George's, as I did not want to get there before the patient. The relatives could go into the family room, while the patient was attended to in resus. I heard the Viking put in a call to St George's and give an ETA of 10 minutes. I drove slowly but still arrived before the patient. The relatives were getting restless, wondering what was going on in the other ambulance.

I was called over by the sister, who asked where the other crew was. I said I didn't know; maybe they had to stop and give more drugs. The sister placated the relatives, while I tried to find out where they were. I phoned Control and asked them to find out, as they had not yet arrived at St George's. She called them over the radio: no response. I gave up and sat in reception.

I could see Jock, who'd we brought in earlier, making a nuisance of himself. He had already annoyed many of the waiting patients, and was starting to get louder. Thirty-five minutes passed and they still had not arrived.

I began to think the worst had happened; maybe they crashed. Another two minutes passed and I could hear sirens, in the distance. That made forty-seven minutes. They finally arrived and I rushed to open the back doors. Jeff gave me a knowing look; a nod. I knew he was desperate to tell me something. They took the patient

into Resus and Jeff handed over to nursing staff, then went to book the patient in.

The patient wasn't on the system as he had been born and lived in Australia. Jeff came out and gestured to me to go to our ambulance, which I had parked well away from the A&E entrance. We sat in the back and closed the doors.

Jeff said after I had left, the Viking had put a call in to St George's, then he burst out laughing and couldn't contain himself. I started to laugh, as it became immediately infectious. I was laughing out loud and didn't know why. Jeff tried to control himself. He said the Viking. had got lost between Morden and Tooting, and that he had left the side door of the ambulance open.

The spinal board had dropped out, hanging half out of the door, as it was securely strapped in. As the Viking drove down a very long road,

the spinal board had hit every car on its journey down the hill. Jeff said he must have hit fifty cars, breaking their side mirrors and scratching their cars. Jeff and the Perv had continued to administer resus, as they both laughed hysterically. I could
picture this all happening, in my mind's eye.

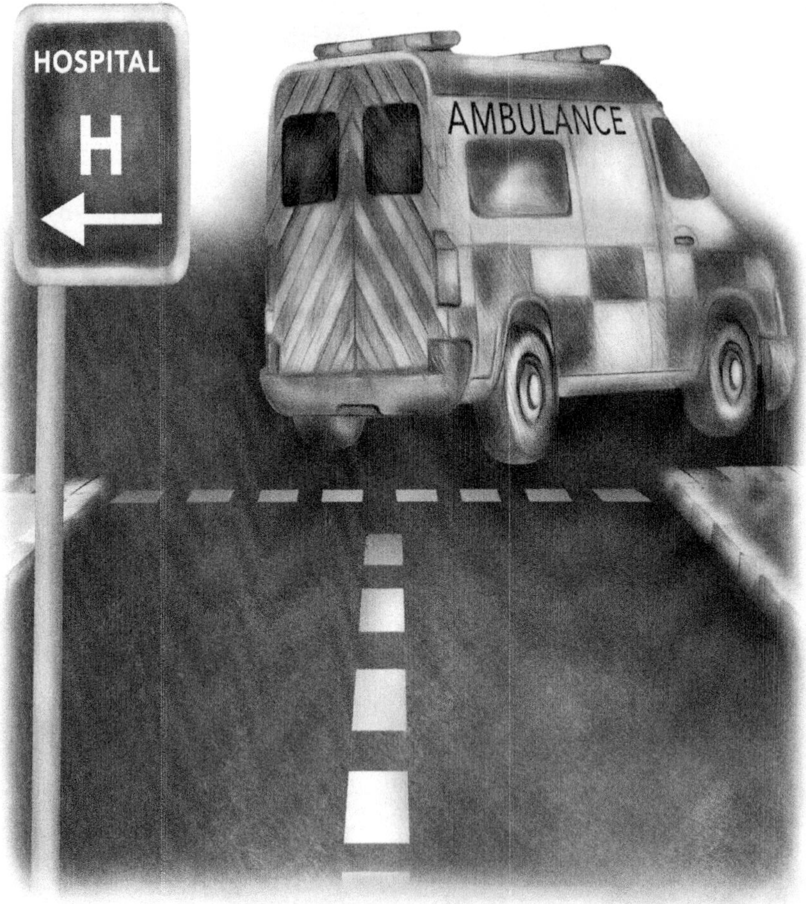
HOSPITAL
H
AMBULANCE

Jeff had shouted, 'Where the fuck you going? It's the wrong way.' He was heading towards Mitcham, totally in the opposite direction. Then he did a ten-point turn hitting two parked cars in the process, causing lots of damage to the cars and his ambulance.

He said the Viking completed his manoeuvre, and drove recklessly, hitting every car he passed on his way to St George's. We laughed so much, I hurt everywhere.

I went out to have a look at the spinal board and the ambulance. The Viking and the Lech came back out. They had to sort out their ambulance and the Norseman had to write an accident report. I couldn't blame him for not wanting to fill that out. I looked at the pair of them

walking towards their ambulance and burst out laughing again.

I just hope the dead Australian, if he was watching from another world, might see the funny side. Jeff made a point of reciting that story to anyone who had not heard it, and every time he told it, he and I both laughed out loud, as much as on the day it happened. I can still laugh now, when thinking about it.

The Ozzie bloke died and I wasn't surprised, if no one carries out some form of CPR, then the patient has no chance, and will die. He may well have stayed dead, for fear of being injured in a fatal crash, with an ambulance crew that was laughing, and a crazy Viking driving.

We went into reception, just as Jock was being wheeled out of A&E. He started swinging his colostomy bag around the waiting area; a disgusting thing to do. He was wheeled out of the hospital grounds and warned not to come back until he sobered up.

Ten minutes had passed. The other two had already left and we were nearing our off- time, just as someone ran into A&E, to say that someone has been hit by a bus. Jeff and I jumped into our motor and drove to the entrance. Jock had fallen out of his wheelchair and into the road. Maybe he had seen a fag and tried to get it, or maybe he'd dropped

something ... anyway he'd fallen out and hadn't been seen by a passing bus, which drove straight over him, followed by a second bus.

It was too late for Jock. He lay there, dead, way past anyone's help, waiting for the

police. The sleepwalker was paralysed from the neck down.

The Lech joined the police. The Viking transferred to Devon. Jeff and I kept laughing, for weeks. Even now, as I

write this, I am in hysterics. No one knows what cards life is going to deal you.

That's why you should make the most of every day, as you never know how much time you have left.

Boy with the moon and stars

You had a cold

...maybe flu,

You walk, to school

Struggle, and Fall Down ...

Dead,

it wasn't your time,

late for school,

 you had excuse.

the boy with the moon and stars.

16. Boy with the Moon and Stars

It was a cold December day, frosty, hot air creating a mist in front of me as I talked. I started work at 7 a.m. and prayed for a reasonably quiet day. I did not want to rush around today, even though that's what my job demanded.

Marc and I checked the ambulance, did our vehicle inspection, then as we drank hot tea, we stocked up on consumables and went back to the mess room. There were two other crews in: six of us. Thank goodness that made us third out. We sat in the comparative warmth of the mess room, one radiator to warm us.

The phone rang. Two crews were out on RT Watch (Radio transmitter listening and waiting for a job) that left us.

At 08.15 the phone rang: ten-year-old male. Suspended. Resus in progress. We were given the address and times.

We had to get to all our jobs in eight minutes or under. We'd be okay with this, as it was just two minutes away and it was my turn to drive. Even our Control's watchful eyes could not track me; I was always off their screen, too fast for them.

We looked at each other and couldn't help thinking that if this job was as given, then it was someone's little boy, dead in the street on a cold December day.

I drove like the devil, my mate clinging onto his seat and the door handle, fearing for his life, lights flashing, sirens blaring, we were on a mission. The only one thing on my mind, the little boy; someone's son.

I swung a left after getting to Battersea Rise. Ninety seconds gone. Drive faster.

Wheels were screeching and smoking. Another left into Trinity Road; a big road; four lanes. I was doing 80 mph when all the lanes merged into one? The traffic stopped. I couldn't drive into oncoming traffic. Fuck! I hit the brakes, knowing I was going to smash into the car in front, and probably take out three more.

My mate was on the floor, bracing himself for the crunch and the smashing of glass, screaming, possible fire and more injuries. I was trying to think of that saying: More haste, less ... If we didn't put ourselves out the kid would die. Three minutes gone.

I stood on the brakes and stopped, just behind the car I was destined to smash.

Suddenly, the sea of traffic moved. Both directions suddenly cleared, as if by magic. I told marc to get up, and stop being a silly wanker. Four minutes gone. The boy had a chance.

I swung a right into Magdalen Road. There they were, a bit further up on the right, resus in progress, by two bystanders. Great! He had a chance.

Four and half minutes had gone, as we thanked and relieved the bystanders, just as our first responder turned up. They are supposed to be our first responders, as they would be given the job first, as a car or motor bike would normally get there before an ambulance. We knew our positions, our jobs: we worked like a Swiss watch, a fucking perfect Rolex. We put the defibrillator on him: no rhythm, flat line. We carried on: great, we got a shockable rhythm. We shocked him ... back to a flat line.

That was the first time anyone had managed to get a shockable rhythm on a paediatric patient anywhere in the world, in the street. It was amazing fact to learn after the event, but not helpful now.

We got the boy into the back and started to strip him. We cut away his puffer jacket.

Feathers flew all around the ambulance, causing us to itch and scratch while carrying out resus. We got him oxygenated, got a line into him, filled him with fluids.

Hi lips were still on the dark side.

Suddenly his mother turned up screaming and crying, I sat her down and explained what we were doing and that we would be going in a minute. Some stupid person hit our ambulance in their eagerness to see what was going on. We carried on with what we were doing, but all of us turned around, and in unison told the person in the car to 'Fuck off!' It was just the adrenaline kicking in.

The mother was still screaming and shouting, all of us itched and scratched because of the feathers. None of us noticed. We did our job.

The first responder said they would put a call in and ask for the HEMS helicopter.

That's what some of our blokes were like, they were there just to make themselves look good, get attention; a few lines in the local paper, maybe even on the TV news. I'm not like that: I don't play games with people's lives. I said, 'No, HEMS would have been given this job first if they were available we're not going to wait another ten or fifteen minutes for HEMS to arrive, and then wait for a police car to go and collect them from wherever HEMS lands. I said ST GEORGES is two minutes away, do you really want to wait?? They agreed with me.

We're going to St George's now.' I strapped the mother in and told her not to worry.

I shut the back doors from prying eyes. Just as I was making my way to the driver's seat, I heard a man screaming, 'Connor, Connor'. It was the boy's father.

I told him to get his car and meet me at St George's, but not to drive like me. I drove with urgency but gently so that they could carry on with resus, I put a call into St George's so they would be expecting us.

The father got to St George's before me. We took the boy into Resus. Then our handover done, we left and let them work on him. I was drained – we all were. It's surprising how much running on adrenalin drains you. As soon as it leaves your body, you're as flat as a pancake … until the next rush.

Time taken: 14 minutes, 30 seconds – well within the golden hour. We had done all we could.

We asked about him every day for two weeks, after they put him into paediatric intensive care. The next time we asked the nurse told us to go up and see him.

He was sitting up, eating his breakfast. Tears welled up into my eyes. His mother came and kissed us both;

she must have kissed us a few hundred times, although it felt like thousands. We knew she was grateful, as was the boy's father, he hugged us like a bear.

We asked the nurse why he had stopped breathing, and learned it was the combination of having an enlarged heart and a common cold. His enlarged heart hadn't been discovered when he was born, but now, with medication, he would live to be an old man, although he would be on meds, the rest of his life. The mother kissed us a couple of hundred more times, then the father turned up, a large man with wild hair and a large beard, he gave me a hug that nearly splintered my ribcage.

We left. Good job done, by all.

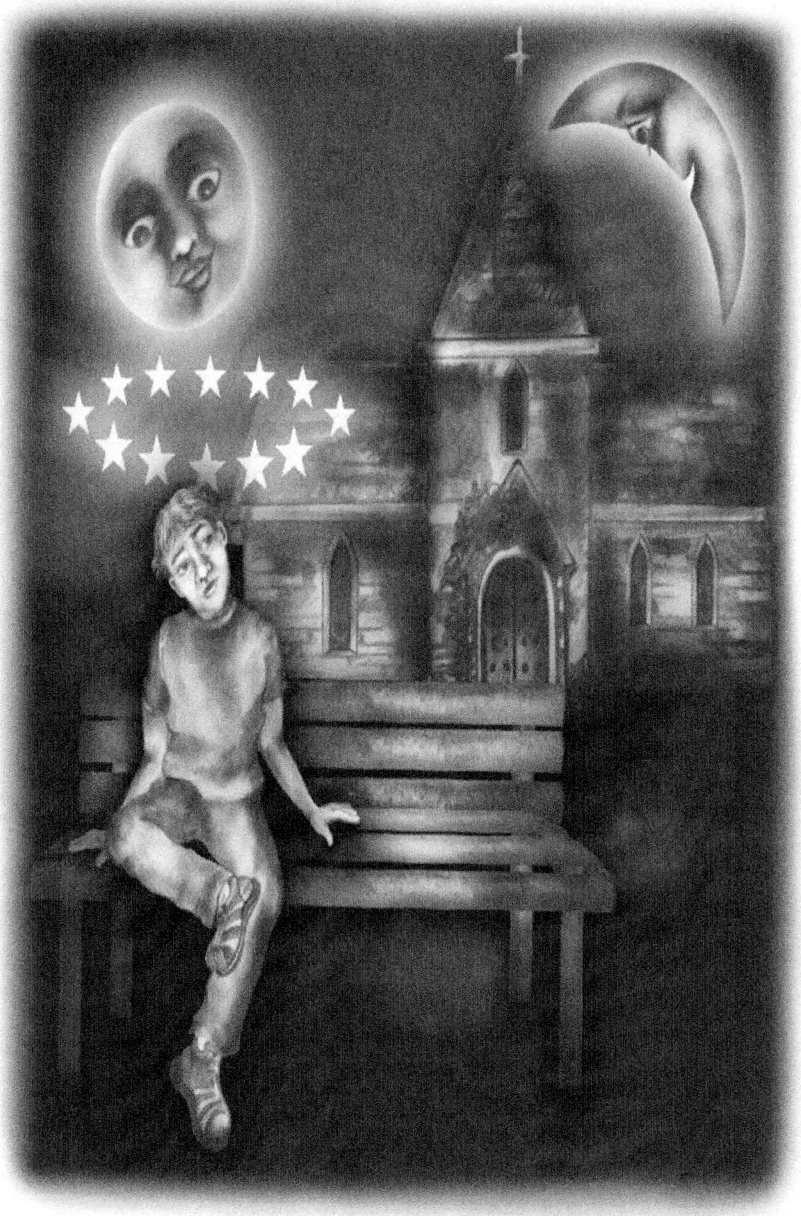

P.S. The reason I called this little chapter 'The boy with the moon and stars' is because Connor was never going to die. He was blessed by some power beyond imagination.

The first bystander that stopped to assist him was a paediatric intensive care nurse from St George's hospital, on her way home from a night shift.

The second bystander that assisted Connor was a consultant paediatrician, from Chelsea and Westminster Hospital, on his way to work. How I wished I had known all this before we got the

job. A combination of everybody doing their jobs saved the little boy from Magdalen Road – the boy with the moon and stars.

The Forgotten

World weary and old

Seen and not seen, in this time

Hugged and kissed by some

Long forgotten

Not missed

To soon to be lain with rose.

17. The Forgotten

The Ambulance Service certainly served up a big slice of pie. We saw the beauty of life being born, with the unfathomable joy of a new mum, and we saw the soul-destroying moments in the faces of people whose friends lay injured, dead or dying. We saw it all in the Ambulance Service, as did they in the Police Service.

One Boxing Day, we were called to a large family gathering. They had all had their dinner and then went to the other room for a sing-a-long, leaving the grandmother in the dining room. She had fallen asleep after dinner, so they decided to leave her there to rest. She was eighty years old.

Eventually they went to wake her, and couldn't, so they called us. She was obviously dead when we got there. They had forgotten about her in the excitement of the party.

We saw the loneliness of the elderly, some of whom had no one in their lives: the sadness in their watery eyes, echoed in the cold, dimly lit room, as they tried to save on heat and power. I thought how selfish we have

become, to not care for our elderly in their twilight years. Yet some of us, in the caring professions, did care, and did make a difference.

We could see it in their eyes, a glint of happiness, when we gave them a bit of our time; showing we cared in that little moment of their history. Who the hell could deny them a bit of time? After all, that's all they had, and it was in short supply.

Was it mainly an affliction of Westerners not to care for their elderly? Did people only want to gain from their relative's death? Who could blame them for leaving their worldly possessions to a cats' home, the Blue Cross, or the RSPCA. They'd had more love shown to them by their pets, than some ever had from their family.

One of the very first things I was given, when I joined the Ambulance Service, was a poem, about the elderly. This has remained with me always. It's by a lady called Phyllis McCormack, or possibly by another unknown person. Its always being reproduced by the health and caring services, and you will see why. Its called, 'Look closer, Nurse'.

I reproduce it here for all to read, and to remember.

Look Closer, Nurse

What do you see nurse?

what do you see?

Are you thinking when you're looking at me?

A crabbbit old woman, not very wise

Uncertain of habit, with faraway eyes

Who dribbles her food and makes no reply?

When you say in a loud voice,

'i do wish you'd try'

 Who seems not to notice the things that you do

And forever is losing a stocking or shoe

Who, resisting or not, lets you do as you will

With bathing and feeding, the long day to fill

Is that what you're thinking,

is that what you see

Then open your eyes nurse,

for you're looking at me

I'll tell you who I am as I sit here so still

As I use at your biddings,

as I eat at your will

I am a small child of ten

with a father and mother

Brothers and sisters who love one another

A young girl of sixteen, with wings on her feet

Dreaming of soon her lover she'll meet

A bride soon at twenty my heart gives a leap

Remembering the vows that I promised to keep

At twenty-five now I have young of my own

A woman of thirty, my young growing fast

Bound to each other with ties that will last

At forty my young sons will now grow and be gone

At fifty, once more babies play around my knee

Again, we know children

my loved one and me

Dark days are upon me,

my husband is dead

I look to the future, I shudder with dread

For my young are all busy, rearing young of their own

And I think of the years, and the love I have known

 I'm now an old woman

and nature is cruel

Tis her jest to make old age look like a feel

The body, it crumbles, grace and vigour depart

There is now a stone where I once had a heart

But inside this old carcass a young girl still dwells

And now and again my battered heart swells

I remember the joys,

I remember the pain

And I'm loving and living life all over again

I think of the years all too few - gone, so fast

And accept the stark fact that nothing can last

So, open your eyes nurse,

open and see

Not a crabbbit old woman,

 look closer, see me.

Every time I had a call to an elderly patient, I would remember that poem and treat the elderly with respect. I once worked with a bloke and we had to take an elderly man home from hospital. It was night-time and the rain was torrential. I helped the old boy into the chair and onto the pavement. The driver pushed the old boy towards his sheltered housing, and I walked behind. The driver pushed the old man into some overgrown bushes: not only was he soaked, but his face was also now scratched. The driver turned around to face me and laughed, as if I thought that was funny. As I was new, I said nothing, but I never forgot his cruel action and never worked with him again.

The summer of 2000 was warm, with some hot and humid weather. A female relief was working with me and we were fourth out. Our first job came at 10.30 for a ninety-one- year-old man. It just said 'unwell'.

The job was in Tooting. When we arrived the front door was open. We went in and I was shocked by the state of his front room. I have been to lots of properties that were a mess, even filthy. I once had to resus a junkie in her flat. She had ten puppies running around her flat and we couldn't see the floor through the dogs' mess. It was a nightmare: no lights; needles everywhere; and we had to resuscitate a junkie. We got her back and conveyed her to hospital. When we finished the job, we had to shower and get a change of clothes.

This old man was emaciated and he was very tall – at least 6ft 4in. He was sitting in his armchair, fresh urine and faeces adding to the pungent air of a hot and humid day. I pulled my menthol rub out and rubbed some under my nose, and Judy followed suit. I went outside and took in a deep breath. Judy followed me out, I told her to wait there until I decided what to do.

The patient's name was Frank. He was softly spoken but unkempt. His clothes were filthy and he stank to high heaven. Next to his armchair, on the floor, was a potty, which was full of urine. The rest of his front room was taken up with newspapers and magazines, piled up to 4 and 5 ft. high. There was a pathway no more than 6 inches wide, which led upstairs, to the kitchen and to the front door. He didn't have home help, but he did have Meals on Wheels.

I took his pulse and his temperature: his temp was high and his pulse was irregular. I asked if he had medication that he took on a regular basis. He told me it was all in the kitchen. I went to find his meds. I cannot begin to tell you how dirty his kitchen was. There were rat or mouse droppings everywhere. I couldn't see his sink, as it was full of plates and saucepans. Even his walls looked like the fungus and mould was moving. He had blood pressure meds, as well as heart meds.

I went back and spoke to Frank and suggested he come to hospital with us. He refused, saying he would rather see his GP. Neither of us were happy to leave him, clearly he was ill, and needed help from Social Services. Judy brought in our pulse oximeter and our defibrillator, and took his observations while I phoned the GP surgery. His GP wasn't in.

I came off the phone and again tried to persuade Frank to come to hospital. Again he refused, and said that he would go to hospital only if his GP said he needed to go. This had become a Catch 22 situation. I phoned Frank's surgery again, in the hope that I could sort something out for our sick patient. The surgery was closed for the next hour. Judy made Frank a hot drink and I decided to phone Social Services and the Council, to see what help I could get for him.

The time was now 13.00, and Frank's house was buzzing with people, although most were outside. I had arranged for Frank to have all his rubbish removed from the house, and for it to be fumigated, and redecorated. The Council and Social Services would supply new second-hand furniture and Frank would not have to pay for anything at all. This would all take place once he was admitted to hospital ... if I could get him there.

He liked the idea of having his house redecorated. I phoned the surgery again and told the receptionist that I needed to speak to Frank's doctor, and that Frank would only go to hospital if he saw his GP. I demanded to know where his GP was, and they told me she was playing golf. I gave them my phone number and asked the receptionist to phone the doctor and ask her to ring me.

I told her to also inform the doctor that we had now been at Frank's for four hours. At

15.00 the doctor phoned me. To say we had words was putting it mildly, I made it clear that it was her duty to forget her golf and come to see Frank, in order to get him admitted to hospital. His doctor turned up at 1600, examined him, and agreed that he had to go to hospital. She left, then we put Frank in our ambulance and left his house at 16.30, after giving a set of keys to the Council.

When we join the Ambulance Service, it is instilled in us that we are in charge of our patients' care, in any way we choose, as long as we are doing our best for the patient. That is

exactly what I chose to do for Frank: I gave him the best care I could. The fact that we returned to station seven hours later did not come into it.

Frank spent two weeks in hospital, and when he returned home it was to a newly decorated house, with new furniture, and with home help twice a day.

I had another job exactly the same, in Wandsworth and I did exactly the same for this elderly man as well. This time the job only took four hours, but in all my years, to only have two jobs like that is not bad going. However, I suspect that in reality there are hundreds more like them. Some of the elderly have nothing, despite being in reasonably good health. They have just have had enough of life, and some pray for death to come and take them.

I hope Frank enjoyed his remaining years of life in warmth and comfort.

I remember the joys,

I remember the pain,

And I'm loving and living, Life, all over again.

Shake, rattle, and roll.

I saw you

before We crashed.

I saw a light

Which blinded

I knew my life was over

I could not speak

I could not think

I felt no pain

As I moved forward

And chewed on glass

Liquid running down my face

The taste of metal, in my mouth,

 Swallowed whole, in my car,

There was no bag to save my face

My chest hit the steering

As my head extended Into screen

I felt no pain I had no control,

Physics Took control

I thought how Odd

That fog Suddenly descended

I felt an odd sensation

As my ribs broke

Both legs broken

A bone Flew up

Landing in my lap

I felt nothing As I wet myself

I felt spread

Like butter on toast

My chest, became disorganised

I felt no pain

Just laboured breathing

I knew I was Leaking ... inside

I felt no pain

Darkness was beginning, to wrap me

In the warmth of Nothingness

still no pain, as my picture faded ...

I did it ... Knowingly

I did it ... willingly

Without malice Or hatred ... I did it

I hit the truck, I'd had enough

Darkness took the fast lane

and overtook my breathing.

18. Road Traffic Collision (RTC)

Three cars were following each other. The lead car had all the booze in the boot. They were off to have a party early one Saturday evening. The three followed each other, into Mead Road, Chelsea, SW10; a straight road which inclined drivers to speed. Coming in the opposite direction, at speed, were two cars racing each other. One was on the wrong side of the road, heading for a collision with the lead car. An impending tragedy unfolded, with a combined impact of at least 140mph.

The lead car swerved on to the wrong side of the road to avoid a head-on collision with the oncoming car. It hit the kerb at speed and flew up in the air. The female passenger in the back was thrown straight through the front windscreen, on impact with the telegraph pole. She landed in the road, smashing her hips and pelvis. She also had fractures to her arm, shoulders and an open fracture to her left leg.

The car continued its forward momentum. Spinning sideways, it hit a lamp post, bringing it down, before it rolled over several times, and then came to a rest on its side. The lamp post crashed down into the road.

The third car nearly ran over the female who had landed in the road. The two passengers in the back of the first car, were both unconscious, with head injuries and upper body fractures.

The car that caused the accident, stopped momentarily, surveyed the scene, then drove off at speed.

The car we were following and which hit the lamp post was caved in at every angle, the driver, George, was unconscious, and trapped in the front. He had multiple fractures, as

well as internal injuries. The other front-seat passenger was screaming in pain. He too had multiple injuries – his name was Edward.

I was in the third car and witnessed everything. I jumped out, while my car was still moving – a stupid act on my behalf – in my eagerness to help my friends. I ran to the nearest house and called the Emergency services.

They were all required. There were no mobile phones in those days. Snow

started to fall and it was getting very cold. We collected blankets from the very generous people in that road. We wrapped jane, our friend with the fractured pelvis, in blankets. Alison she stayed with her.

I and my mates Ben and Andy tried to free the others. Oil and petrol had covered the area around the car, and we were afraid it would catch fire.

That was my introduction to an RTA (or RTC, which is what they now call it). The scene was carnage, the police and fire men turned up in force. After thirty minutes, two ambulances turned up, and took the three rear-seat passengers to St Stephen's Hospital.

George was still unconscious when the brick-heads freed him.

No more ambulances had turned up. Edward was still trapped. I lost count of how many times he said 'Help me'. I could do nothing for him; he needed to be cut free. I knew he was seriously injured: his voice became fainter; he stopped moaning.

Two more ambulances turned up and they loaded George into one of them. Edward's legs were crushed in the squashed metal of the car. The top half of his body was hanging out of the car. I supported him, until they eventually freed him. His voice became a whimper. I knew he was dying, unless he got to hospital quickly.

Exactly one hour after the crash, Edward was freed, strapped up and put in the ambulance. My heart lifted after feeling totally useless. The ambulance driver could not start the ambulance. Everybody there got behind and pushed it until we got it going. It was now eighty minutes after the crash, and he was finally on his way.

The rest of us made our way to St Stephen's Hospital and sat in the waiting room. We wanted news of the injured five. A doctor and nurse came out of Resus and addressed us. We were now a group of thirty people in the waiting room. News travelled fast.

The doctor told us that Edward had died: his spleen had been ruptured and had other severe internal injuries. We were all as broken as George's car. We all cried, thirty-nine years later. I can still see it all.

All the attention had turned to George, who had become the focus of blame, especially by the police.

Many years later I joined the Ambulance Service, where I had to attend many more RTCs. Many were serious, and many more were nothing more than a reason for a financial claim.

One night we got a call to a chap, who had been knocked off his bike on Wandsworth Roundabout. That was one roundabout that was bad to negotiate in a car, never mind a pushbike. He had been hit by something big and had multiple injuries, but his main injury was his fractured skull. He had blood and cerebrospinal (CS) fluid coming out of his ears.

He had been wearing headphones and listening to music on his iPod. The vehicle that hit him had left. There were no witnesses. We blued him to St George's, where he later died.

On another late shift we got a call to Trinity Road; a long straight road, where people tended to speed, on a dual carriageway. The vehicles concerned had been heading north, towards Wandsworth Roundabout. I could not work out what had happened. There were two cars involved: one had hit a tree, which had stood its ground for 200 years or more; the other was smashed to pieces and had finished up on its roof. Three bodies had been thrown out of the car that hit the tree, and had all landed on the grass verge. There were two still in the back of that car. The other car had three passengers.

The accident happened at about 23.00, on a weeknight, so there wasn't much traffic on the road. We were first on scene. It was a nightmare, carnage. I called Control and said to make that ten ambulances, as well as sending the police and the Fire Service, if they weren't already on their way. We were overwhelmed. When the police and firemen arrived, we split up in order to triage all the patients.

Out of the eight patients, five were unconscious. The Fire Brigade set up lights and started to free those trapped. At least we were now organised, so that when the other ambulances arrived, we could direct crews to those in most need. I could hear the comforting sounds of more ambulances on their way.

Access had now been gained to all patients, but the scene was unreal: a plethora of emergency staff, working in organised chaos, to save lives. That was our goal. Crews split up. Everything was working like clockwork. The Duty Officer found us and I said that patients need to be taken to three different hospitals, as there were a lot of seriously injured people.

I stuck with my unconscious patient. We immobilised him and put him on a spinal board. You had to factor in the worst possible injuries and treat for the worst. My patient had internal injuries, an open fracture to his right leg. He had a Glasgow Coma Scale (GCS) of 5 it's a measurement of consciousness, 3 is deep coma or death, you reach your numerical value by testing each of their responses, for eye, verbal, and motor responses, moving of a limb. My crew-mate was elsewhere, and I now had a chap from Fulham helping me with my patient. I put in a Blue Call to St George's, and told the Duty Officer where we were going. I drove as my Fulham comrade didn't know the way. I had lost my ambulance so used someone else's. We all ended up doing that; patients were the priority.

We were there in five minutes. With our patient in resus, we grabbed a coffee and our breath, then set about cleaning the ambulance.

Six of the eight patients died within the week, including ours. It was very difficult at times not to be despondent about our work. Imagine how many people those deaths would affect. We could not get away from the fact that we dealt with people's misfortune, and that only some had a positive outcome. It was the nature of our job.

I just wondered how much space I had left in the dark recesses of my mind, in which I could file away the worst of my jobs. The trouble was that there were too many ... and I was running out of filing cabinets.

One afternoon while having coffee at St George's, we heard Control calling us. We had been called to another job at 15.00, on a hot Thursday afternoon. The job was given as: female hit by bus. NFD. We were only one minute away. When we got there

the woman was trapped between two buses, and was standing upright, moaning in pain.

She wasn't my first patient to be hit by a bus. My first had been a big man, who had stepped in front of a moving bus while chatting on his mobile – his fault. He was thrown 30 feet, and that isn't an exaggeration. When we arrived, he was conscious, without pain, and a GCS of 15.

I said, 'Sorry, Dave, but I have to cut off your leather jacket, to examine you.'

He looked at me, and said, 'No, you fucking won't!' And with that, he stood up, took his jacket off, walked to the ambulance and lay on the stretcher. Then he said, 'Now you can examine me.'

We checked him all over and found nothing, but because he had been thrown so far, I insisted that he went to hospital with us. We took him to Chelsea, and two hours later we watched him walk out, not even wearing a plaster, He was built of rock.

Another time in Clapham, a child had been walking with his nan, and his mother was on the other side of the road. His grandmother had let go of his hand, and he had spotted his mother and ran towards her. The five- year-old was hit by a bus, which went over him. The bus driver could do nothing. We could do nothing. We could not have recognised him as a human. It was devastating.

The lady trapped between the buses was called Gloria. She was squashed, alive, but she was going to die. The fact that she was squashed was keeping her upper body functioning, but as soon as the buses were removed, her awful internal injuries would cause her blood pressure to plummet and she would die.

No one wanted to move the bus to free her. I didn't want the bus moved, so I made my feelings known. I wanted to call her family, so that she could see and speak to them, probably for the last time before she died, as that was going to be the outcome.

But we couldn't get near her, until the bus was moved, so we got everything we needed, ready. Just then the fire men turned up. I told them my thoughts, but I was out-voted, as someone made the decision to move the bus. A fireman moved it, and we went in with our equipment, put her on our stretcher and into the back of the ambulance. She was immediately unconscious.

That was one day I was glad to be driving. Had I known we were going to get a job like that, I would have stayed home. I put in a call to St George's, less than a minute away. She had massive internal injuries. We took her into Resus and the doctors did what they could. She had lacerations to her spleen and liver, but she died of cardiac tamponade, (her heart bled and filled the heart cavity, which stopped the heart functioning) – an extreme medical emergency, with rarely a good outcome, if ever.

19. The Worst Day Shift

At 06.00 on a Friday, James and I sat down with a drink, after checking our vehicle. Unfortunately, we were first out, but I did not want to rush today; I wanted an easy day. I was in no mood for any crap, from anyone. The phone rang immediately as the printer spewed out a job. I exchanged initials with Control. We had a twenty- year-old maternity, first pregnancy.

This was good, because I did not fancy delivering a baby at six in the morning. The job was in Balham, not far, and she was due for a St George's delivery. Great; an easy run, straight road.

We left. James drove. We arrived to find a group of four males waiting for our arrival, jumping up and down, beckoning us to hurry up. The young lady met us at the front door. Her waters had just broken and she said her contractions were between 3 and 4 minutes. I made her lie down on the stretcher.

All of those anxious blokes, and not one of them joined us. I assumed one of them might be the father, but maybe I was wrong. I made her comfortable and propped her up. Then I said that I needed to take a look, just to see if the baby's head was crowning. She must have anticipated this, as she wore no underwear. I gave her instructions to open and close her legs on my command. I did not want to be caught out, so I asked James to put in a Blue Call to St George's: birth imminent; ETA 5 minutes.

James drove, a bit slow for my liking, maybe he was doing it deliberately, but I told him to drive faster,

I told the young lady to open. She opened her legs at my command. I called to James to drive faster,

Open. Close. Drive faster. This is how it went until we got to St George's: Open.

Close. Faster.

James was pissing himself with laughter as all he could hear was Open, Close, Faster; Open, Close, Drive Faster; Open, Close, Drive Faster. I began to laugh as well, and wondered if my wife would have taken my commands as willingly as this lady.

We got to St George's in six minutes, and by the time I had booked her in and James had taken the trolley back to the ambulance, her baby had been delivered. We grabbed a drink and sat in the ambulance.

I greened up ready for another job: a fifteen-year-old girl with abdominal pains, in Blackshaw Road, the same road as St George's. We were always going to get this, as there were no other ambulances here. We got to the job in a minute.

The girl was in the bathroom, with her mother, with the father in the front room, moaning and anxious, I said to the mother through the door that we needed to see the young girl. The door was unlocked and the mother came out, followed by his daughter and a baby. The daughter had been pregnant, the mother and daughter had kept it quiet from the father, until the very last minute. The father started shouting at his daughter. I tried to calm him down, while James put her in the ambulance with her mum. We left as quickly as we had arrived, much to the annoyance of the girl's father, who was left at home, alone and cursing. I hoped he would come around in a few hours, as I was worried about the young girl.

It was now 08.25, and the day had not gone the way, I had wanted it to. I greened up and thought we were going back to station, but how wrong I was. We were given a job to a sauna: an unconscious thirty-eight-year- old man. James drove at speed. I had never seen or heard of the place.

When we arrived, I realised what this place was: a place for homosexuals, where gay men could meet and get together. As we walked in, we both felt uncomfortable. There must have been sixty eyes staring at us.

The patient was lying face-down on the floor. 'How long has he been unconscious for?' I asked. No one answered. There was a bottle of amyl nitrate next to him. We had no choice but to start resus. He had a towel wrapped around him. Everyone was dressed in small towels, music blaring, drinking alcohol or coffee.

It was a surreal scene. The building was full of Greco-Roman pillars and a small pool, surrounded by tables with sun umbrellas ... all indoors. We proceeded with our protocols for resus, although looking back on it, I wished I had asked for police attendance. It was obvious something untoward had occurred. We blued him to St George's, unconscious: thirty-eight- year-male; cardiac arrest; CPR in progress. We both knew he had been down for a while.

The hospital ran through their protocols and eventually called it.

I greened up and we managed to get a return to station. We arrived on station to find out that no one else had been out yet. We both fancied some toast. I think most NHS staff lived on toast, peanut butter and marmite. James made tea, I made toast. I noted to James that at least we were now fourth out.

The printer had made taking jobs by pen and paper obsolete. Our printer took a deep breath, made a noise and whirred into action and printed three jobs one after the other. The other crews grabbed their jobs and spoke to Control in turn, four times and with initials.

'Fuck!' I said. 'That makes us first out already.'

We didn't have to wait long before we copped another job in Balham: a taxi to St George's Maternity, and that's what it was – a taxi ride, I expected St George's to send her back home as she was early, her waters were intact and if there were no beds she would be going home.

I laughed to myself, as she would have to pay for a proper taxi if she returned home. I settled back in my chair and took details and looked at her maternity pack. The couple were both in their early twenties: she was white and he was black; both English. He started to chat about politics. I joined in with relish, as I do love a good natter about politics.

I complained about the British and the American Governments, about their foreign policies, about how much trouble they had caused worldwide. He obviously felt comfortable in my company and said, 'Wait till you see what happens in July.' His partner shushed him up and I never took much notice. He whispered to me "July, wait and see"

We dropped them off at maternity, I wished them well and left. I finished off my paperwork while I told James of our conversation, which he had heard some of.

I never thought any more of it – until 7/7 happened.

James drove while I greened up, as we were given a job to Battersea: a drunk assaulted; head and facial injury. I wondered if it was Little and Large, as it was their area, in a road near to where they lived. We arrived, and as I suspected, it was Little and Large, the difference being that for once it wasn't Tim who had got a beating; it was Roger.

I asked James to see to Roger, clean him up and see if he needed the hospital, while I took Tim away and asked him what had happened. Tim told me that Roger had tried to take his money, so he'd punched him in the bollocks, as I'd told him to, and when Roger fell down in pain, Tim started to kick and punch him.

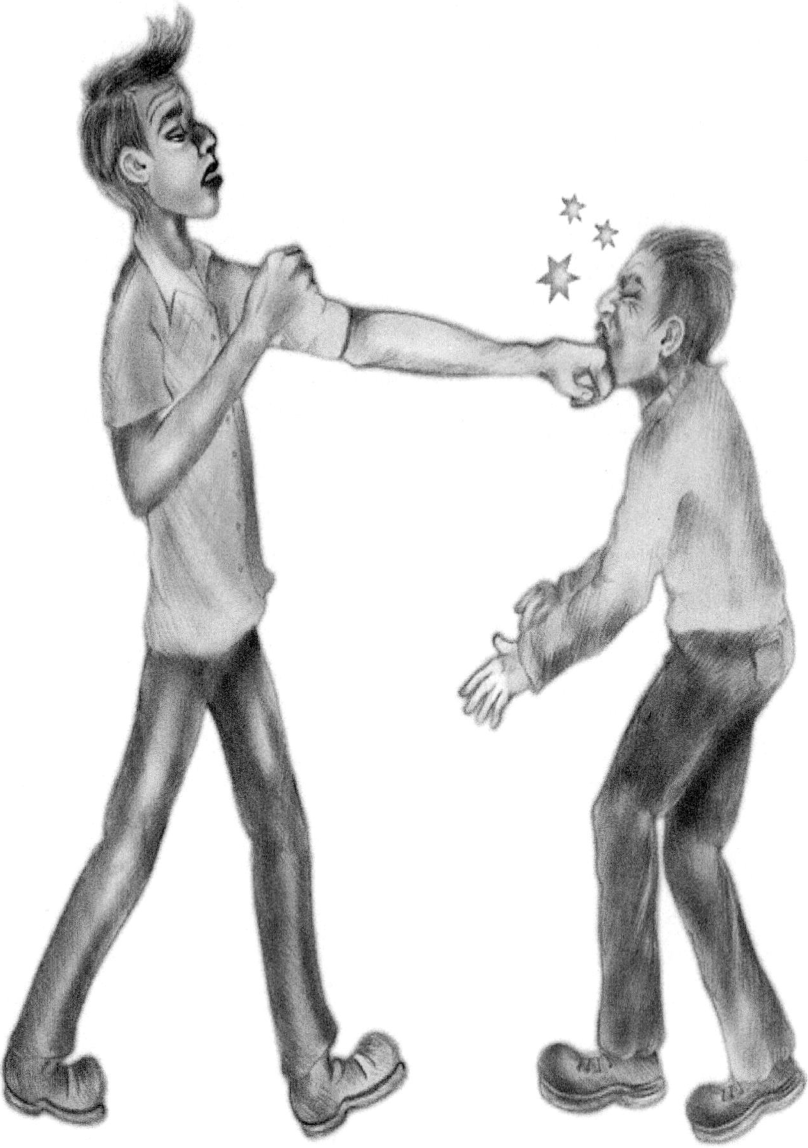

Tim thanked me for the advice I gave him and we shook hands. I made him walk up to Roger and asked him to apologise, which he did. Roger didn't need the hospital. We walked away as they shook hands, hoping maybe now they might treat each other as proper friends and human beings.

I greened up, and we got a call to Nine Elms, for another drunk, on the other side of the bridge, past Battersea Dogs Home, near the fruit and veg market. I spotted him and told James to wait in the ambulance, as I did not want to waste too much time with him. I jumped out and opened the back doors, pulled him up off the floor and got him onto a chair in the ambulance. He wanted to lie down on the stretcher, but I told him that was only for sick people, not alcoholics. He called me a 'Bastard cunt foreigner.' I said, 'You're as foreign as me', as he was Asian. He spat at me, and I told him if he did it again I

would call the police. He gobbed at me, so I asked James to get the Old Bill, I crawled into the front, to get some distance from him.

He attacked me, trying to kick me, as he lunged forward with his left foot. I kicked his foot and this caused him to fall over, then I just put my feet on him till the police came and took him away.

I finished my paperwork. We only had five hours left. I greened up and we got a job to assist a lady to the toilet. When we got there, we were led up to a small bedroom. The lady had her bed against the wall long ways, and there was a commode near the bed for easy access – or so we thought.

There was a shelf, which ran the whole length of her 6-foot bed, filled with chocolates, sweets, crisps, muffins, Coke, other cakes, and bars and bars of chocolates. I left the room: the smell of urine was destroying my nasal passageways. I had to put some Vicks under my nose. I gave some to James who smothered it outside and under his nostrils.

We went back in, gloves on, as I stood on her reinforced bed and we heaved her up, and dropped her onto the commode. I'm surprised it held her. I don't know why they called us, as it was obvious she wet her bed most of the time. We heaved her back onto her bed, all 24 stone of her, and left.

We got out into the early evening air, and gulped it in in large amounts, and just for good measure I put myself on oxygen, pure O2. I filled in my paperwork, while James breathed in some O2.

Unfortunately, we still had time for two or three jobs. I greened up and we got a call to behind Clapham Train Station, for a male; query stabbed; query unconscious/dead.

James drove fast, invisibly pushing everyone out the way, and we got there in five minutes. I took the tool kit and ran toward a small crowd, while I left James to get the stretcher. There were five people hanging over this male, but no police yet. I checked him over: he was cold and waxy; his chest was hard; his pupils were fixed and dilated.

I told everyone to move away, as this was now a crime scene. The police arrived just as we were printing off a strip on our defibrillator: he was flat line and had been dead for a few hours. He was just in his early twenties, and as far as I could see, there was just a single stab wound, near the left side of his chest. A large bowie knife was under his rucksack, but there was nothing else in his bag.

We gave the cops our details and left.

I finished off my paperwork and greened up. We copped a job in Clapham; female 28; laceration to head; shouting on scene; police had been called. James got us there in three minutes. It looked like our Control was getting slightly better at giving jobs to the nearest crew.

We walked up to a large flat. A very butch lady answered the door. She was extremely red in the face and looked like she wanted to hit someone – it wasn't going to be me.

I asked, 'Where is the patient?' as she led us into the front room.

Well to say that James and I were surprised was a complete understatement. We were both shocked and flabbergasted. It took me a moment to speak, as I surveyed the room and I asked the patient to tell us what had happened. They'd had a lovers' tiff, and the lady that let us in, had lost her temper and thrown a glass ashtray at her lover's head, causing a small laceration. She didn't need to go to hospital. I got James to dress the wound, while I started doing my paperwork.

The injured lady was beautiful, she was wearing her work clothes – skimpy leather knickers, a leather something that just about covered her boobs, stockings and suspenders. The room was full of sex gadgets: a large stainless steel pole, leather masks, ropes, whips, nipple clamps with a battery and stocks. There were also lots of little black balls that looked

like squash balls, just a bit bigger. My imagination ran. I wondered if they played a racquet sports here as well.

The police came just as I finished my paperwork and I gave them a quick lowdown. I could see they too were shocked and amazed. We wished them well and left.

We had time for two jobs, or for one involved job. I greened up, expecting the worst.

We were given an urgent job to Colliers Wood: she needed to be seen, and admitted, by a doctor for surgery. James parked and I had a horrible feeling I knew this address. I waited to see if I was right, rang the bell, and went in as the door was open.

'Bloody hell!' I said under my breath. It was her. I used to pick her up when I worked in the Patient Transport Service. She was huge; 'fat' is a serious understatement. She was bigger than our previous patient. I remembered picking her up with my partner on PTS.

I put my arm around her waist, to ease her into a chair. Since I'd last seen her, she'd put on maybe another 7 stone. She sat in a reinforced wheelchair. I went and spoke to her and she gave me her doctor's letter to read.

It took both of us to push her wheelchair. I told James to stop and I asked Lesley, our patient, if she had a tape measure.

She said, 'What do you want that for?'

I said, 'Because your wheelchair won't fit through your door.'

I knew we wouldn't be conveying her. It was now 17.00. I phoned the Council, to see if they could get someone down to remove the door and door frames. No joy there.

I asked James to radio Control and tell them we need another crew, with a PTS ambulance and a large hospital chair. I asked Lesley if she had any tools and she told me to go to a shed outside.

I found a hammer and bolster and started to take down her flat, bit by bit. I took the door frames off, but her chair still wouldn't fit. The door came off, as I got myself in a sweat. At this rate we were going to be late off. The other crew would have to go to St George's first to get a chair and I doubted if they would use blue lights to get there and back to us. I had to start chiselling away at one side of the wall. I measured again. James was laughing at how farcical this job was. If she had been a cardiac arrest, we wouldn't have been able to convey her. We would just have done the paperwork and written her off.

I finished measuring and there was enough room for the wheelchair to be pushed out.

The other crew got to us at 18,10 and we left them with the problem, after I telephoned Control to get them to find someone who could put her door back on. I didn't fancy telling them over the airwaves that I had taken her flat apart.

We drove back to Lavender Hill, where we both slumped into our armchairs, before going home. The next day we had a phone call, from the crew that had taken over our job. They had taken took her to St George's, where she was admitted, but no one would risk their backs to get her onto a hospital bed. So, they called the firemen, as they were the only people in the emergency services that were insured for their backs.

20. Worst Night Shift

We started at 19.00, James and I. There were four crews on. The others were out when we started our shift. Ten minutes in and we were out. Our first job was to an RTA, near Brixton Station.

I drove. It was one of those days when I didn't want to listen to some of the rubbish spoken in the back. I could listen to some music when driving, and tonight I was in the mood for classical music. We got to the RTA. The car had crashed into a lamp post, but there was no damage.

James went to the driver, and shouted to me to get the stretcher.

The driver's arm had been severed, but was still connected by sinew and a couple of blood vessels. The driver's side was covered in blood, as was the driver's shelf and the door well. This was no normal RTA. We got him in the back and blued him to St Thomas's.

James did what he could, but it was useless. There was no blood left in his body to keep him alive. He had been attacked with a machete, and we guessed he had then tried to drive himself to hospital before passing out.

James completed his paperwork, while I mused over the job. The whole point of this job was to make a difference, but the only difference we'd made to him was

taking a dead body from point A to point B.

James greened up and we immediately got a job to Balham. James asked if there was anyone closer, but their reply was that we were the only ones available. It was for a seventy-year-old female, unwell. I drove there at a steady 50 mph, as the roads were full of traffic. We got there in nine minutes and we were met by the husband, who told us that Martha was waiting in the upstairs bedroom.

I brought a chair and blanket with me, and James

rapped on the bedroom door. No answer. We went in, and to our horror the 12ft × 10ft bedroom was plastered in blood. I have never seen a room like it. It might as well have been painted red ... badly. In the time since the call had been made her aneurysm had ruptured. She was dead.

James asked me to call Control and ask for the GP and police to attend, as that was protocol. I went downstairs to Alf, as I had to tell him that it was too late to help his wife.

He looked through me, not understanding my words. I said, 'Alf, Martha, your wife, is dead. We're just going to get your doctor to come out. Shall I call someone for you?' He called his eldest son who lived locally, and we stayed until the GP and the police officer arrived.

James completed his paperwork and greened up. It was going to be a long night. We got another job, to Tooting, I wondered if this patient was going to be alive: a forty-year-old male; abdominal pain.

We parked at the front, but I was informed to go to the rear entrance, so I did. We were met and led through the rear part of a building that was double-height and looked like a hanger. It housed a dormitory for what I'd guessed to be illegal immigrants. There were at least twenty mattresses on each side – at least forty people in one room. Fucking disgusting!

I followed them up some stairs, which led to the front of the building. There were bubbling pots in a galley kitchen, a tiny kitchen. James went to see the person with the abdominal pain. They could see St George's from their window; that's how close they were.

'Tight bastards!' I said under my breath. I looked around the kitchen. They were cooking curry for Sainsbury's. There must have been a contract, and whoever had that contract was subbing it to these filthy fools. I asked and he confirmed it was for Sainsbury's. There were empty cartons and packaging everywhere, all for Sainsbury's.

It was the filthiest kitchen I had ever seen, and if Sainsbury's had known, they would have been worried sick, to think their customers were eating from this pigsty. Unbelievable. We took the patient to St George's and made him walk to the ambulance. There was no way I was going to carry him. After we dropped off the patient we grabbed a coffee.

I told James what I had seen, and who they were making curries for. He pulled a sickly face at my information. I now wished I had taken a couple of photos and reported it to the council. It seems odd to me that you wouldn't report this when you reported other things. After all, this kind of thing could potentially result in deaths just as much as malpractice by medical professionals.]

It was a stormy night, the rain tumbled from the sky continuously, and the wind became fierce. James greened up and we were given a job to Kingston: an unconscious twenty-year- old female. I put my foot down and drove fast. With my route worked out and planned in my mind, I hit the accelerator.

I don't know why, but I had a bad feeling about this job. All my lights were on as I drove like lightning. I didn't know this road, but it was opposite Kingston Hospital. As we were going to turn right, James looked in the hospital car park, where he saw six ambulances parked up, their crews chatting.

We got to the house and were met by the mother; the father was away on business. The mum took us up to Mary's room. She was as white as a sheet. James pinched her ear lobe: no reaction. I touched her face: she felt waxy. I pulled the sheets off her. She was naked and the bed was full of blood. She had cut her femoral artery and lain in bed until she passed away. I caught the mother just as she fainted.

Her mother had been out at work and then for a coffee with a friend. She'd come home, and eventually looked in her daughter's bedroom, where she'd found her unconscious. Her daughter had suffered with depression.

I called James to help me lay her down on her own bed, then I called Control for police to attend. This was a black night; blacker than the blackest of nights I could remember, and now I was glad it was pissing down. I wanted it to rain. I looked on the rain as tears for mankind, especially for the patients we had tonight.

She was an only child. I sat with the mother who presently started to shed tears, consistent with the weather. I just held her hands. I didn't want to ask her any questions, as she would have lots from the Old Bill. The doorbell rang and James let the police in. I was glad one was a woman, as some men couldn't or wouldn't show any emotion or affection.

I told James I would wait in the ambulance. At times like these I wished I smoked, then regretted that stupid thought. James came out after twenty minutes. He had finished his paperwork inside. I watched as the ambulances all seemed to get a return from Kingston Hospital.

James greened up and we got a return. This was going to be the calm before the storm, and it was a full moon, so this was just the beginning of a long night.

I drove up the A3 towards Wandsworth, ensuring we would not get a job, at least not until we had reached station. The station was full when we greened on. There were two reliefs working from Wimbledon Hill. They told us they'd had a job where a tree had fallen on a car, trapping two blokes. The car exploded and caught fire. They both died.

They asked James about our night. He didn't want to say much, neither did I. We all seemed to be lost in our own thoughts.

One of our crews had been to a shooting. Police were on scene. The patient had been shot in the face and our crew thought he was dead, but as they were leaving, a cop said, 'He's blowing bubbles.'

They looked again. He was bubbling air through blood, so they checked his carotid pulse again. It was faint, but it was there, so they had to convey him to Tommy's.

It seemed to be a bad night for everyone. I had no appetite. I didn't want a drink. I think I wanted another job just to get out of this mess room, to break away from this heavy foreboding silence. I think I even longed for a drunk – that would do.

The printer whirred into action. We could see everyone waiting to see how many jobs it spewed out of its revolving mouth. The phone rang, and one after the other we all left: four in, four out. We got what I wished for – a drunk. I recognised the address. He was a fucking pain in the arse. He would be really lucky if I didn't shoot him between the eyes with my spud gun.

He was outside the address. They must have kicked him out, like rubbish. I know that drunks have problems, I understand that, and I understand all about addictions, how it's in your genetic make-up. I do have sympathy and feeling for some of them, but at the same time, they need to help themselves. He was a dead weight as we struggled to get him in the ambulance. He fell onto the stretcher and into a happy deep sleep, snoring. I was glad I wasn't not in the back listening to that.

As I was going to the front, Control put out a request for anyone who could assist with a suspended baby. I looked at James. We both had the same idea. I pressed in and said that we were not far from the job. They asked me if we had picked up yet. I replied 'yes', and she said to continue with our journey.

We were two minutes from that baby. James was as pissed off as I was. How could they be so stupid? It was like we didn't have a patient on board; it was like we had a fucking sleeping lodger.

I sat in the front and put some classical music on to soothe my nerves. I never realised what James was up to. It was quiet in the back and he was sitting right behind me, which was unusual. James gave our drunk a short back and sides, chopped off most of his hair. I laughed so much I nearly wet myself.

He gave the drunk a proper haircut, and I mean a proper haircut, bagging the hair in a vomit bag, I was tempted to put it in his pocket, but I thought better of it. That cheered us both up. Fifteen minutes later, we heard that the suspended baby job had just been given out. I thought, too fucking late. That baby had no chance now. The drunk had stopped that baby from having a chance at life, and as for Control, I blamed them as well.

That renewed our anger towards the drunk and now I wished I'd shot him with my spud gun. We had a coffee and did paperwork. It was still raining and the roads were becoming flooded. James greened up, as Mozart's Flute and Harp Concerto started to play: one of my favourite pieces, very relaxing, a proper chill-out sound.

I drove back towards Lavender Hill, when James asked me about a job I'd had a couple of months earlier, in Wimbledon. It was on a Monday morning. A family had recently moved into their new home. The husband went out to the garage, to clear some remaining rubbish. He swept up and bagged up the rubbish. He saw a fire extinguisher in the far corner, picked it up and shook it. The extinguisher exploded like a long-forgotten bomb, and ripped out his throat and part of his face, missing the main artery. When we got there the woman was jumping up and down on the spot, pulling at her hair, I wondered if this was a normal reaction, as I have had lots of jobs where people pull at their hair.

We scooped him up and flew to St George's. Control had given us the job as a fire extinguisher 'going off', not that it had 'exploded'. Anyway, the chap lived. He spent four months in hospital, and had to have several operations on his face.

He held a party and invited everyone – all but the two who'd saved his life. That's just how it was: we were wanted in times of emergencies and then forgotten about. It was the same for all the emergency services, we are forgotten until we are needed for an emergency.

Another time I remember, we shocked a woman's sister back to life. The sister had seen her

drop down dead and did nothing, except call us. Probably shock. The woman made a full recovery, no thanks to her sister. In the end we came to expect nothing from the public; not even a thank you. The only people that were different were the elderly: they always appreciated what we did for them. James grunted in agreement. I put Mozart on again.

We greened on station. The police were there and I wondered why. We'd all had serious jobs tonight. They wanted to leave a message for the crew who'd been sent to the car, with passengers, that a tree fell on and subsequently caught fire, burning them alive.

They told us to let the crew know that both victims were drug dealers and that the police had been after them for months for pushing hard drugs onto kids. There's something to be said for karma.

It was still raining, the wind was still blowing and I still wasn't hungry.

We were second out, I pulled up another chair and rested my legs on it, glad no one was in the mood to play practical jokes, as I think I would have hit them, or just shot them with my spud gun.

It was now 0200 and the printer came alive: two jobs. We were out again: a sixty-year-old female, unwell.

The others got a stabbing in Clapham, whereas we were off to Fulham. I put on some Sigur Rós I was feeling melancholic. I loved their music and had heard it so often that I could sing along with it, although, not knowing what I was singing.

I drove to Fulham, and James knocked on the door. Doris answered and we followed her in. She sat down, while James asked her questions: she had no history of illness; she didn't want to make a fuss; and she didn't really want to go to hospital. All her observations were fine.

Some other crews would have been happy to have left her and arrange for a doctor to see her. But I wasn't happy to leave her. After all, she had called us, so something was wrong. And years earlier I'd had a watershed moment with a patient exactly like Doris: all observations had been fine; ECG fine; no previous illnesses – the only thing was she had a tiny ache in her tummy, and was a bit anxious. It turned out she was having a heart attack.

We took Doris and when we went back another day, it had indeed been a proven MI – myocardial infarction (heart attack). Doris had only shown signs of being anxious with a tummy ache.

James greened up and we got a return. I played some more Sigur Rós. We were approaching station, when they called us and gave us a job to Lambeth: young female sitting on pavement, please investigate. This road was difficult to find, but we found the lady after fourteen minutes. She smelt of alcohol and was unresponsive. I got the stretcher and we loaded her up, and took a closer look. She was still very unresponsive, but she was alive – barely.

I put a call into Tommy's and we arrived in 5 minutes. We took her into Resus and went to grab a coffee. We thought the lady had got drunk, sat down to rest and fallen asleep. When we asked after her in Resus, they said that had we not got to her when we did, she would have been dead, as she was hypothermic. She must have been outside for ages to get into that condition.

The night was relentless with calls. Now we had one to Wimbledon Theatre, from Tommy's. There was no use arguing. I drove fast, no music, and James pushed himself back into his seat. I think I was in the wrong profession; I should have been a racing driver.

We arrived in twelve minutes to find one person standing near our patient. She called us. Our patient was behind a large car, a Range Rover, which was squashed up against him. James checked him: he was unresponsive, pupils fixed and dilated. He had been sheltering under an overhang from the rain. There were no lights at this side of the car park. The driver must have parked their car as far back as he could go, and crushed the homeless man, who was probably asleep, killing him.

I went to the ambulance and radioed for the police. It was another crime scene. We left after giving them our details. This was bad news for us, as we still had time for one job. James greened up, and we got a return. Two minutes from station, Control called and we were diverted to a road not far from where we were. It was for a lady on the floor, unable to get up. If this was just an assist, it was a perfect job. We could do this job, and drive back to station, green on, and be last out.

But as luck went, we had none – it seemed to be in very short supply for us. We were met by a man in his forties who was mentally slow and showed us to his mother. She was on the floor, completely covered in faeces and urine. The son had placed a glass of milk and a sandwich next to his mum. I went and got several blankets. If we were not careful it would be a messy job.

James came with me, so that we could bring the stretcher in as well. There was no way of knowing how long she had been on the floor. When we freed her hand that she had been lying on, it was flat, like a cardboard cut-out of a hand. It had become malleable.

We double-gloved and set about rolling her up in our blankets. Then we wrapped her up and put her on our stretcher. I spoke with her son, asked if she had any medication, but I never got very far with him. I looked around the large room, and said, 'Guess what, James?'

'What?' he said.

I said, 'A female crew was here two weeks ago: one works at Putney Hill and the other at our station. They said that the mother had refused hospital.' Now the mother could not have signed the PRF (patient report form), so I took it with me. We had to blue her into St George's. She was seriously dehydrated and starved of food.

Why did they leave her on the floor? Were they in a rush to get home, or was it because she was covered in faeces? Either way they never took care of this patient, there was evidence of food and drinks, that she had been fed while on the floor, as well as days of faeces and urine. These two should never have been in the job. How could our patient and her son slip through our care system? Someone must have known about them, and it would never have happened if the female crew had done their job properly. As for our patient's hand, she could have lost it.

I was seriously disappointed in some of our staff. I did not know if I should let this go. After all I had informed my superiors about the activities of our staff and the lack of proper management by our so-called superiors and senior management, and it never seemed worthwhile. However, I still reported it, but it fell on deaf ears.

James did a thorough handover and we made sure they got the help they needed from Social Services. That's all we could do. We drove away from St George's and greened up at

07.00 exactly. The only thought in my mind was my lovely bed.

Epilogue

I left the service in 2009 and moved to Devon. I joined the Devon ambulance service working in their control room. This time I wasn't attending calls, I was answering them, and I never needed a tool bag, or a big ambulance, just a computer.

The jobs were similar, and no two days were the same, there were just less calls, and no stressful driving to negioate to get to calls. You still had a certain degree of satisfaction from helping patients, and possibly helping to save a life in what may be someone's darkest hour. It's a worthwhile job, and its rewarding in many ways, its just when you look at some statistics that you can become disillusioned, like only 1 in every 10-15 calls involves someone in a potentially life-threatening situation.

I now spend my time painting and creating mixed media art, as well as writing poetry.

LIVE A GOOD LIFE.

IF THERE ARE ANY GODS AND THEY ARE JUST,
THEN THEY WILL NOT CARE HOW DEVOUT YOU HAVE BEEN,
BUT WILL WELCOME YOU
BASED ON THE VIRTUES YOU HAVE LIVED BY.

IF THERE ARE GODS, BUT UNJUST, THEN YOU SHOULD NOT WANT TO WORSHIP THEM.

IF THERE ARE NO GODS, THEN YOU WILL BE GONE, BUT WILL HAVE LIVED A NOBLE LIFE, THAT WILL LIVE ON IN THE MEMORIES OF YOUR LOVED ONES.

MARCUS AURELIUS.

Printed in Great Britain
by Amazon